HeritagE BUILDERS

Family Night Tool Chest

Book 1

An Introduction to Family Nights

Creating Lasting Impressions for the Next Generation

Jim Weidmann and Kurt Bruner

with Mike and Amy Nappa

ChariotVICTOR
PUBLISHING
A DIVISION OF COOK COMMUNICATIONS

This book is dedicated in love
to my wife, Janet,
for being my best friend and a godly mother,
and to my children—Joshua, Jacob, Janae, and Joy—
for being my inspiration and a source of many blessings.
Without all of your love, patience, encouragement, thirst, and support,
this book would not have been possible.
—J.W.

Victor Books is an imprint of ChariotVictor Publishing,
a division of Cook Communications, Colorado Springs, Colorado 80918
Cook Communications, Paris, Ontario
Kingsway Communications, Eastbourne, England.

HERITAGE BUILDERS/FAMILY NIGHT TOOL CHEST, BOOK 1
© 1997 by Kurt Bruner and Jim Weidmann

First edition 1997

Edited by Liz Duckworth and Mandy Finkler
Design by Bill Gray
Cover Illustration by Guy Wolek

ISBN 0-7814-0096-1

Printed and bound in the United States of America
01 00 99 98 97   5

Heritage Builders/Family Night Tool Chest, Book 1, is a Heritage Builders book, created in association with the authors at Nappaland Communications. To contact Heritage Builders Association, send email to: Hbuilders@aol.com.

Contents

Family Nights about Basic Christian Beliefs

Family Nights about Christian Character Qualities

Family Nights about Wisdom Life Skills

The Heritage Builders Series

This resource was created as an outreach of the Heritage Builders Association—a network of families and churches committed to passing a strong heritage to the next generation. Designed to motivate and assist families as they become intentional about the heritage passing process, this series draws upon the collective wisdom of parents, grandparents, church leaders, and family life experts, in an effort to provide balanced, biblical parenting advice along with effective, practical tools for family living. For more information on the goals and work of the Heritage Builders Association, please see page 118.

Kurt Bruner, M.A.
Executive Editor
Heritage Builders Series

☉ Introduction

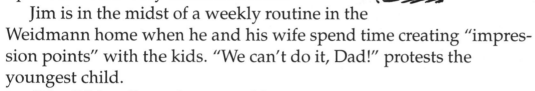

There is toothpaste all over the plastic covered table. Four young kids are having the time of their lives squeezing the paste out of the tube—trying to expunge every drop like Dad told them to. "Okay," says Dad, slapping a twenty-dollar bill onto the table. "The first person to get the toothpaste back into their tube gets this money!" Little hands begin working to shove the peppermint pile back into rolled up tubes—with very limited success.

Jim is in the midst of a weekly routine in the Weidmann home when he and his wife spend time creating "impression points" with the kids. "We can't do it, Dad!" protests the youngest child.

"The Bible tells us that's just like your tongue. Once the words come out, it's impossible to get them back in. You need to be careful what you say because you may wish you could take it back." An unforgettable impression is made.

Impression points occur every day of our lives. Intentionally or not, we impress upon our children our values, preferences, beliefs, quirks and concerns. It happens both through our talk and through our walk. When we do it right, we can turn them on to the things we believe. But when we do it wrong, we can turn them off to the values we most hope they will embrace. The goal is to find ways of making this reality work for us, rather than against us. How? By creating and capturing opportunities to impress upon the next generation our values and beliefs. In other words, through what we've labeled impression points.

The kids are all standing at the foot of the stairs. Jim is at the top of that same staircase. They wait eagerly for Dad's instructions.

"I'll take you to Baskin Robbins for ice-cream if you can figure how to get up here." He has the attention of all four kids. "But there are a few rules. First, you can't touch the stairs. Second, you can't touch the railing. Now, begin!"

After several contemplative moments, the youngest speaks up. "That's impossible Dad! How can we get to where you are without

touching the stairs or the railing?"

After some disgruntled agreement from two of the other children, Jacob gets an idea. "Hey, Dad. Come down here." Jim walks down the stairs. "Now bend over while I get on your back. Okay, climb the stairs."

Bingo! Jim proceeds to parallel this simple game with how it is impossible to get to God on our own. But when we trust Christ's completed work on our behalf, we can get to heaven. A lasting impression is made. After a trip up the stairs on Dad's back, the whole gang piles into the mini van for a double scoop of mint-chip.

Six years ago, Jim and his wife Janet began setting aside time to intentionally impress upon the kids their values and beliefs through a weekly ritual called "family night." They play games, talk, study, and do the things which reinforce the importance of family and faith. It is during these times that they intentionally create these impression points with their kids. The impact? The kids are having fun and a heritage is being passed.

☙ intentional or "oops"?

Sometimes, we accidentally impress the wrong things on our kids rather than intentionally impressing the right things. But there is an effective, easy way to change that. Routine family nights are a powerful tool for creating intentional impression points with our children.

The concept behind family nights is rooted in a Biblical mandate summarized in Deuteronomy 6:5-9.

> *"Love the Lord your God with all your heart and with all your soul and with all your strength. These commandments that I give you today are to be upon your hearts. Impress them on your children!"*
> ***How?***
> *"Talk about them when you sit at home and when you walk along the road, when you lie down and when you get up. Tie them as symbols on your hands and bind them on your foreheads. Write them on the doorframes of your houses and on your gates."*

In other words, we need to take advantage of every opportunity to impress our beliefs and values in the lives of our children. A growing network of parents are discovering family nights to be a highly effective, user friendly approach to doing just that. As one father put it... "This has changed our entire family life" And another dad . . . "Our investment of time and energy into family nights has more eternal value than we may ever know." Why? Because they are intentionally teaching their children at the wisdom level, the level at which the children understand and can apply.

◉ truth is a treasure

Two boys are running all over the house, carefully following the complex and challenging instructions spelled out on the "truth treasure map" they received moments ago. An earlier map contained a few rather simple instructions that were much easier to follow. But the "false treasure box" it lead to left something to be desired. It was empty. Boo Dad! They hope for a better result with map number two.

STEP ONE:

Walk sixteen paces into the front family room.

STEP TWO:

Spin around seven times, then walk down the stairs.

STEP THREE:

Run backwards to the other side of the room.

STEP FOUR:

Try and get around dad and climb under the table.

You get the picture. The boys are laughing at themselves, complaining to Dad, and having a ball. After twenty minutes treasure hunting they finally reach the elusive "truth treasure box." Little hands open the lid, hoping for a better result this time around. They aren't disappointed. The box contains a nice selection of their favorite candies. Yeah Dad!

"Which map was easier to follow?" Dad asks.

"The first one." comes their response.

"Which one was better?"

"The second one. It led to a true treasure." says the oldest.

"That's just like life." Dad shares. "Sometimes its easier to follow what is false. But it is always better to seek and follow what is true."

They read from Proverbs 2 about the hidden treasure of God's truth and we end their time repeating tonight's jingle—"Its best for you to seek what's true." Then they indulge themselves with a mouthful of delicious candy!

☺ the power of family nights

The power of family nights is two fold. First, it creates a formal setting within which Dad and Mom can intentionally instill beliefs, values or character qualities within their child. Rather than defer to the influence of peers and media, or abdicate character training to the school and church, parents create the opportunity to teach their children the things that matter most.

The second impact of family nights is perhaps even more significant than the first. Twenty to sixty minutes of formal fun and instruction can set up countless opportunities for informal reinforcement. These informal impression points do not have to be created, they just happen—at the dinner table, while driving in the car, while watching television, or any other parent/child time together. Once you have formally discussed a given family night topic, you and your children will naturally refer back to those principles during the routine dialogues of everyday life.

If the truth were known, many of us hated family devotions while growing up. We had them sporadically at best, usually whenever our parents were feeling particularly guilty. But that was fine, since the only thing worse was a trip to the dentist. Honestly, do we really think that is what God had in mind when he instructed us to teach our children? As an alternative, many parents are discovering family nights to be a wonderful complement to or replacement for family devotions as a means of passing their beliefs and values to the kids. In fact, many parents hear their kids ask at least three times per week

"Can we have family night tonight?"

Music to Dad and Mom's ears!

Keys to Effective Family Nights

There are several keys which should be incorporated into effective family nights.

MAKE IT FUN!

Enjoy yourself, and let the kids have a ball. They may not remember everything you say, but they will always cherish the times of laughter—and so will you.

KEEP IT SIMPLE!

The minute you become sophisticated or complicated, you've missed the whole point. Don't try to create deeply profound lessons. Just try to reinforce your values and beliefs in a simple, easy to understand manner. Read short passages, not long, drawn out sections of scripture. Remember: The goal is to keep it simple.

DON'T DOMINATE!

You want to pull them into the discovery process as much as possible. If you do all the talking, you've missed the mark. Ask questions, give assignments, invite participation in every way possible. They will learn more when you involve all of their senses and emotions.

GO WITH THE FLOW!

It's fine to start with a well defined outline, but don't kill spontaneity by becoming overly structured. If an incident or question brings you a different direction, great! Some of the best impression opportunities are completely unplanned and unexpected.

MIX IT UP!

Don't allow yourself to get into a rut of routine. Keep the sense of excitement and anticipation through variety. Experiment to discover what works best for your family. Use books, games, videos, props, made up stories, songs, music or music videos or even go on a family outing.

DO IT OFTEN!

We tend to find time for the things that are really important. It is best to set aside one evening per week (the same evening if possible) for family night. Remember, repetition is the best teacher. The more impressions you can create, the more of an impact you will make.

MAKE A MEMORY!

Find ways to make the lesson stick. For example, just as advertisers create "jingles" to help us remember their products, it is helpful to create family night "jingles" to remember the main theme—such as "It's best for you, to seek what's true" or "Just like air, God is there!"

USE OTHER TOOLS FROM THE HERITAGE BUILDERS TOOL CHEST!

Family night is only one exciting way for you to intentionally build a loving heritage for your family. You'll also want to use these other exciting tools from Heritage Builders.

The Family Fragrance: There are five key qualities to a healthy family fragrance, each contributing to an environment of love in the home. It's easy to remember the Fragrance Five by fitting them into an acrostic using the word "Aroma"—

A—Affection
R—Respect
O—Order
M—Merriment
A—Affirmation

Traditions: Meaningful activities which the process of passing on emotional, spiritual, and relational inheritance between generations. Family traditions can play a vital role in this process.

The Right Angle: The Right Angle is the standard of normal healthy living against which our children will be able to measure their atttitudes, actions, and beliefs.

Impression Points: Ways that we impress on our children our values, preferences, and concerns. We do it through our talk and our actions. We do it intentionally (through such methods as Family Nights), and we do it incidentally.

Please see the back of the book for information on how to receive the FREE Heritage Builders Newsletter which contains more information about these exciting tools! Also, look for the new book, *The Heritage,* available at your local Christian bookstore.

@ How to Use This Tool Chest

Summary page: For those who like the bottom line, we have provided a summary sheet at the start of each family night session. This abbreviated version of the topic briefly highlights the goal, key scriptures, activity overview, main points, and life slogan. On the reverse side of this detachable page there is space provided for you to write down any ideas you wish to add or alter as you make the lesson your own.

Step-by-step: For those seeking suggestions and directions for each step in the family night process, we have provided a section which walks you through every activity, question, scripture reading, and discussion point. Feel free to follow each step as written as you conduct the session, or read through this portion in preparation for your time together.

A la carte: We strongly encourage you to use the material in this book in an "a la carte" manner. In other words, pick and choose the questions, activities, scriptures, age appropriate ideas, etc. which best fit your family. This book is not intended to serve as a curriculum, requiring compliance with our sequence and plan, but rather as a tool chest from which you can grab what works for you and which can be altered to fit your family situation.

The long and the short of it: Each family night topic presented in this book includes several activities, related scriptures, and possible discussion items. Do not feel it is necessary to conduct them all in a single family night. You may wish to spread one topic over several weeks using smaller portions of each chapter, depending upon the attention span of the kids and the energy level of the parents. Remember, short and effective is better than long and thorough.

Journaling: Finally, we have provided space with each session for you to capture a record of meaningful comments, funny happenings, and unplanned moments which will inevitably occur during family night. Keep a notebook of these journal entries for future reference. You will treasure this permanent record of the heritage passing process for years to come.

@ 1: Unseen Power

Exploring the visible power of our invisible God.

Scripture:
- John 1:18—No one has seen God.
- John 4:24—God is Spirit.
- Luke 24:36-39—Jesus returned as a real Being.
- 1 Timothy 1:17; 6:15b-16—God is invisible.
- Genesis 1:1—God created the earth.
- Romans 1:20—Creation reveals God.
- Psalm 19:1-6—Nature declares God's existence.
- Psalm 14:1—Those who don't believe God are foolish.

ACTIVITY OVERVIEW		
Activity	Summary	Pre-Session Prep
Activity 1: Forces Are With You	Experiment with unseen forces of nature.	You'll need one balloon for each family member, a ball, one or more refrigerator magnets, and Bibles.
Activity 2: Creative Creator	Examine creation for evidence of God.	Video or picture books of creation, and Bibles.
Activity 3: Not a Chance!	Compare creation to a task dependent on chance.	Paper, pencil, and Bible.

Main Points:

— God is invisible, real, and powerful.

— Though we can't see God, we can learn about God through creation.

— To deny God's order and creation is to deny God's existence.

LIFE SLOGAN: "Just like air, God is there!"

Make it your own

In the space provided below, outline the flow and add any additional ideas to guide you through the process of conducting this family night.

Prayer & Praise Items

In the space provided below, list any items you wish to pray about or give praise for during this family night session.

Journal

In the space provided below, capture a record of any fun or meaningful things which happened during this family night session.

WARM-UP

Gather family members and explain: Today we're going to begin a new tradition in our home called "Family Night" to help us learn more about God. To do this, we'll all be participating in experiments, projects, activities, discussions, and more. In fact, there's no telling what we might do while we learn about God!

Establish the Ground Rules:

Take a few moments and have each family member share what he or she hopes to get out of this series. Then ask all family members to agree to some basic guidelines for family nights. For example, you might suggest that everyone promises to participate in all activities and discussions, and that all involved promise not to be unkind or put down one another.

Open in Prayer:

When everyone is ready, have a family member pray, asking God to help everyone in the family understand more about Him through this time. Then move on to activity #1.

ACTIVITY 1: Forces Are With You

Point: God is invisible, real and powerful.

Supplies: You'll need one balloon for each family member, a ball, one or more refrigerator magnets, and Bibles.

Opening question: How can God be real when we can't see him?

Share: Let's do some experiments to examine other things which are real, but that we can't see . . .

Activity: Stand on a chair and stretch your arm out at shoulder level, with your palm open and facing the floor. Tell family members to examine closely the area between your palm and floor and to report what they see there. Affirm kids for their responses.

Share: There's something important between my hand and the floor that we can't see—gravity! Even though we can't see it, we can see the effect it has.

Place a ball in your outstretched palm, and then drop it to the floor. Ask the children what they saw. Then drop the ball again and have the children quickly pass their hand through the path of the falling ball. Ask what they felt. If children are interested, have them do the same thing. Explain: **Just because we can't see or feel gravity, it doesn't mean it does not exist. It's the effects of gravity we see, like how it pulls this ball to the floor—and keeps us on the ground.**

Age Adjustments

FOR OLDER CHILDREN, **check out a library book with further experiments on air or wind, gravity or magnetic forces. Lead your family in one or two of these more elaborate tests of invisible forces.**

FOR YOUNGER CHILDREN, **focus only on the balloon and magnet experiments given here. Let children enjoy chasing the deflating balloons and playing with the magnets.** SPECIAL NOTE: **Balloons can pose a choking hazard to young children. Keep balloons and their fragments out of small children's hands and mouths!**

Activity: When children are ready, pass out the balloons, and have each person inflate his or her balloon. (Younger children may need help with this.)

Share: We can't see the air we blow into these balloons, but the power of that air is so strong, it can stretch the elastic of these balloons. Though we cannot see the air, we can sure see the effects of the air (what it does). Watch what else the balloon can do!

Release the opening on your balloon and let it fly around the room. Have family members take turns releasing the balloons and watching them fly around the room. Just for fun, inflate the balloons again and again, seeing which balloon goes the highest and the farthest.

Activity: Have the children take turns pulling magnets off the refrigerator and replacing them. Test how far away from the refrigerator can you hold the magnet and have it still pull toward the refrigerator instead of dropping to the floor.

Place two magnets on the floor and see how far away from each other they must be before they rush together. Or, use the positive and negative ends to push magnets away from each other. Be sure each family member has an opportunity to feel the magnetic push and pull.

Share: When the magnet sticks to the refrigerator or pushes away, we can't see the magnetic force, but we can feel and watch its *effects*.

Ask:

- **Even though you can't see it, do you believe in air?
  Gravity? Magnetic force? Why or why not?** *(Answer: Yes!
  You can see and feel it.)*
- **How is that like believing in God?** *(Answer: God is real, even
  though He is invisible.)*

Share: Let's look at what the Bible has to say about this. *(Depending
on the age of your children, you may want to have them look up the
following passages or you might reference and interpret them for the
children.)*

 Read Bible and discuss:

John 1:18: We learn that **no one has seen God the Father.** He
made Himself known through Jesus, His son. Even Moses and other
Old Testament characters never say God, they only saw the "Glory
of God").

John 4:24: God is a Spirit, not limited by time and space like we
humans are. That's why He can be everywhere at once.

Luke 24:36-39: Jesus' heavenly body was not just a restored
human body like ours, **He is real** and able to appear and disappear
as He did here behind locked doors.

**Share: Just as gravity, air, and magnetic force are invisible, God is
invisible. But also like these forces, God is real, powerful, and active
in our lives.**

ACTIVITY 2: Creative Creator

**Point: Though we can't see God, we can learn
about God through creation.**

 Supplies: You'll need a video or picture
book from the library featuring the beauty of nature. Look for materials display-
ing national parks or parts of the world
with spectacular mountains, waterfalls,
greenery, and so on. Or find examples of
unusual fish, lizards and other creatures
God's created. You'll also need Bibles.

Opening Scripture: Read Genesis 1:1
aloud together.

Age Adjustments

FOR OLDER CHILDREN, plan a hiking
excursion in a local outdoor area. Visit
mountains, deserts or even a large
park, and explore the beauty and creativity of God firsthand! Take your
Bible along and read Psalm 148
together in the middle of God's creation.

FOR YOUNGER CHILDREN, visit the zoo
or a pet store. Marvel at the incredible
variety found in creation. The colors,
the sounds, the textures of various
animals is incredible! Talk about how
creative and powerful God must be to
have made all these animals.

Share: In the beginning, God created everything out of nothing. Man can't do that, can he? Let's take some time to look more closely at the world God has made.

Activity: Show the video or pictures you've gathered, taking time together to comment on and appreciate the beauty of what God has created.

Share: The Bible tells us even more about God's creation.

Read Psalm 19:1-6 and Romans 1:20 aloud together.
Psalm 19:1-6—David points out that God reveals Himself through His creation.

Romans 1:20—Through general revelation, nature shows us God's wisdom, power, and perfection in detail.

Question:
- **How do you think the sky tells us about God?** (*Answer: It shows us God's vast, huge, awesome reach because we are all just a speck in comparison.*)
- **How is God's power shown through creation?** (*Answer: There are things man cannot control, like the weather; we cannot control how hot it gets, how much it snows, the power of earthquakes or tornadoes, etc.*)
- **How does creation around us let us know God is God?** (*Answer: God has a purpose and order for His creation. God gave animals instincts that help them survive, like the birds that know when and where to fly to escape the cold, and the lyons that know how to hunt for food. God also made the earth rotate and be positioned a certain distance from the sun so that there are seasons. These facts show us that God knew what He was doing when He created the earth and ordered the way things work.*)

Share: We can't see God, but we can learn a lot about Him through the things He has created—including us humans!

Take a moment to affirm your family members by completing this sentence about each person: **"God created (name), and through (name) I am reminded that God is (blank)."** For example, "God created Tony, and through Tony I'm reminded that God is full of joy!" Be sure to say something affirming to each child and to your spouse. If family members feel comfortable, have them do the same thing. Then move on to the final activity.

ACTIVITY 3: Not A Chance!

Point: To deny God's order and creation is to deny God's existence.

 Supplies: 10 small pieces of paper, a pencil, and a Bible.

Share: There are some people who don't believe in God, and they explain creation as happening simply by chance. Let's try a project to see if that's true.

Activity: Have a family member write the numbers 1 through 10 on individual pieces of paper. Mix the numbers in a pile, then explain that each person will get an opportunity to line up the numbers using only random chance to do it.

Invite each family member to toss the numbers into the air and see how many they can get to land in proper order (1,2,3 and so on). Let each person take several turns, then congratulate the person who got the most numbers in order.

Share: The chance of these numbers landing on the ground in order is very small, if not impossible for you and I! The way the numbers landed when we threw them is called random chance. Some people think the world was created by random chance.

 Read Psalm 14:1 aloud.

Question: Why do you think the Bible calls these people fools? (*Answer: The person who can't see the evidence of a Creator God in the mountains and sunsets is a fool!*)

Activity: Have the children now line up the numbers in different orders that you provide (1-10, even then odd numbers, etc.)

Share: If we use our hands to line up the numbers properly, we no longer rely on chance for them to be orderly. In the same way, the

world was created and works in an ordered way because our invisible God created and directs the world.

WRAP-UP

Gather everyone in a circle and have family members take turns answering this question: **What's one thing you've learned about God today?**

Next tell kids you've got a "Life Slogan" you'd like to share with them. Explain: **A Life Slogan is a little phrase, or jingle, we can use to help us keep in mind what we've learned.**

Life Slogan: Today's Life Slogan is this, "Just like air, God is there!" Have family members repeat the slogan two or three times to help them learn it. Then encourage them to practice saying it during the week so they can talk about it at your next family night session.

Close in Prayer: Allow time for each family member to share prayer concerns and answers to prayer. Then close your time together with prayer for each concern. Thank God for listening to and caring about us.

You might want to start a family prayer journal so that prayer requests can be kept track of and answers can be recorded as evidence of God's working.

Age Adjustments

This activity may be too abstract for younger children. As a substitute activity you might try this: Take a family photograph and place it under a sheet of clear plastic. Then give children markers or crayons and allow them to draw on the photograph. When the children are finished, remove the plastic to show the picture is unharmed.

SHARE: Just as the unseen plastic protected the family picture, our unseen God has power to protect our real family.

Additional Resources:

Where is God? by Karen King (ages 4-8)
This is God's World by Charlotte Stowell (ages 1-4)
Have You Seen the Wind? by Jan Godfrey (ages 4-8)

⊚ 2: Jesus Gets What We Deserve

Exploring how Jesus took our punishment.

Scripture:
- John 3:16—God loves us so much, He sent Jesus.
- Romans 3:23—We have all sinned.
- Romans 5:8-9—Jesus took the punishment we deserve.
- Romans 6:23—We deserve to die as punishment for our sins.

ACTIVITY OVERVIEW		
Activity	Summary	Pre-Session Prep
Activity 1: On Target	Shoot for a target, and compare this to sin.	You'll need a target of any kind, items to shoot at it, and Bibles.
Activity 2: Just Desserts	Earn a reward for work done.	You'll need a job to do, a dessert reward, and Bibles.
Activity 3: Family Court	Simulate a courtroom and judge various activities from the past week.	You'll need a Bible, a bath robe and a list of things your children have done wrong in the past week.

Main Points:

— We all Sin.

— We deserve punishment for our sin.

— Jesus took the punishment we deserve.

LIFE SLOGAN: "When Jesus died that day, He took my sins away!"

Make it your own
In the space provided below, outline the flow and add any additional ideas to guide you through the process of conducting this family night.

Prayer & Praise Items
In the space provided below, list any items you wish to pray about or give praise for during this family night session.

Journal
In the space provided below, capture a record of any fun or meaningful things which happened during this family night session.

WARM-UP

Open with Prayer: Begin by having a family member pray, asking God to help everyone in the family understand more about Him through this time. After prayer, review your last lesson by asking these questions:

- **What did we learn about in out last lesson?**
- **What was something fun about our last session?**
- **Do you remember the Life Slogan?**
- **Have your actions changed because of what we learned? If so how?** Encourage family members to give specific examples of how they've applied past learning.

ACTIVITY 1: On Target

Point: We all sin.

Supplies: You'll need a target and items to shoot at the target. For example, a basket and ball, a yarn circle on the floor and paper airplanes, or a soap target drawn on a window and suction darts.

Activity: Set up your target and let family members take turns shooting at it. When anyone (including you) misses the target, loudly call out, "Sin!" Don't explain your actions, but continue to do this over and over as everyone is playing. After everyone has had several turns at target practice, put aside the toys.

Ask:

- **How did it make you feel when I kept calling out "Sin!"?**
- **Why do you think I did that?**

Allow family members to share their thoughts.

Share: The word "sin" means to miss the mark, or miss the target. So every time you missed the target, I was reminding you of sin! The Bible explains more about this.

Read: Romans 3:23 together in your Bibles.

? Question:
- **What does it mean to fall short of the glory of God?** *(We cannot be holy or sinless.)*
- **How is this like missing a target?** *(We miss the mark; our aim is off.)*
- **What target are we aiming for in life?** *(To be like Jesus.)*
- **How do we know when we hit this target?** *(We obey His commandments.)* **How do we know when we miss?** *(We fail; we sin.)*
- **What are examples of ways we sin?**

If family members seem to be focusing on sins like murder, robbing a bank or other deeds they've never done, turn their attention to more likely sins such as lying about doing their chores, hitting a sibling, sneaking a dollar from dad's wallet, cheating on a test at school and so on. Also include sins adults are likely to commit such as gossiping, not telling the whole truth or being greedy.

- **The verse says, "All have sinned . . ." Who do you think this means?** *(Every person.)*
- **Do you know of anyone who has never sinned?** *(Only Jesus never sinned.)*

Share: The target we're aiming toward is to be just like Jesus. Just like us, He lived here on earth, played, worked, and was tempted to do wrong things. But unlike us, he never did anything wrong! He never missed the target! You, me, and every other person ever born sins and misses the target, but Jesus never did!

Now we need to find out what happens because of all the sinning we do.

ACTIVITY 2: Just Desserts

Point: We deserve punishment for our sins.

Before this session, think of a simple task family members can do together that will only take five or ten minutes. For example, raking the yard; washing, drying and putting away the dishes; or washing the car. Be sure to gather any supplies you'll need for this activity beforehand. You'll also need Bibles and a dessert reward (such as candy bars or ice cream).

Age Adjustments

Adjust the work activity according to the ages of your children. OLDER CHILDREN may undertake a more difficult task, while simply sweeping the walk is a tough job for younger ones. If ages in your family vary, divide the tasks so each child has a part. For example, YOUNGER CHILDREN may gather larger twigs while parents and older children rake leaves in the yard.

Share: There's a small job that needs to be done, and I've set aside a reward for everyone who helps in doing this job.

Activity: Explain the job and the reward, and set about doing this together.

If a family member chooses not to help, remind this person that they're also choosing not to have the reward. Use their decision in the later discussion, pointing out the consequences of our decisions, whether negative or positive.

After the work is done, get out the dessert and eat it together.

Discuss these questions as you eat:
- **Do you think this dessert was a fair reward or payment for the job we did?**
- **What other types of rewards or payment do different family members get for their work?** *(This could include payment at work, grades on report cards, special honors or awards in sports or clubs, and so on.)*
- **What kind of payment do we get when we do something nice for someone?** *(This may be only a good feeling inside or the secret joy of helping another.)*

Share: Payment or rewards we get for our work are called wages. It's what we earn. We often earn some kind of payment when we do good things. On the other hand, we might also get "payments" when we do bad things.

- **What kind of wages does a robber or murderer get after being caught?** *(They go to jail or are put to death.)*

Share: Just like we can earn good things by good actions, we can earn bad things by bad actions. The Bible makes this clear in Romans 6:23a.

 Read Romans 6:23a together.

Question:
- **What does this verse mean?** *(The price we pay for sin is death.)*

• **What do we earn for our sins?** *(We die.)*

Share: The Bible says we deserve to be punished for our sins. Fortunately, God made a way for us to not be punished. Jesus took the punishment we deserve.

ACTIVITY 3: Family Court

Point: Jesus took the punishment we deserve.

 Supplies: You'll need a bath robe and a list of bad deeds family members have committed during the week. List infractions small and large, including things such as not doing chores, arguing, slamming doors, and so on.

Share: As we're learning about sin and punishments, I'm going to act as a judge and determine the punishments you all deserve. Let's set up this room as a court room. While we're doing this, I suggest you all think about what you've done wrong recently and prepare your defense!

Activity: Place chairs in a row with a table in front, and chair for the judge behind the table. Put on a bath robe (as your courtly attire) and pull out your list of bad deeds.

Call the room to order and announce that court is in session. Ask everyone to be seated and call each child up one at a time. Read the appropriate wrong-doings and ask how the child pleads. Allow children to use other family members as witnesses in their defense and to explain their actions if they like.

When all cases have been heard, announce which parties are guilty and which (if any) are innocent. Then pass judgment on each individual.

Share: You all knew what you were doing was wrong, but you did it anyway. This means you deserve to be punished!

Activity continued: Name the punishment each family member will receive. This may be a spanking, a fine to be paid, loss of privileges, extra chores, and so on. Tell family members these fines must be paid immediately.

As family members are about to begin their punishments, stand up, take off your robe.

Share: Because I love you all so much, I'm going to take your punishments for you.

At this time, you must pay the appropriate fine, be spanked, agree to the extra chores or whatever was previously determined. You, the judge, *must actually take the punishment, not just waive it.* (You might want to consider this as you're planning what punishments to inflict!)

Discuss the activity after the judge has taken the punishments:

- **How did you feel about our family court?**
- **What were you thinking and feeling as your wrong actions were discussed?**
- **Did you think the punishment the judge ordered was fair? Why or why not?**
- **How did you feel about the judge taking your punishment?**

Share: We already know that we deserve to die for all our sins. But someone else took our punishment so we don't have to.

Read all of Romans 6:23, as well as John 3:16 and Romans 5:8-9.

Question:
- **What do these verses tell us about our punishment?** *(We deserve to die, but God made a way to save us.)*
- **Do you think it's fair that Jesus took your punishment?**
- **What do these verses tell us about God's love for us?** *(He loves us enough to make a huge sacrifice.)*
- **Jesus did this for us as a gift. What does that mean to you?**
- **What do we need to do to get this gift?** *(We only need to accept it.)*
- **How does this make you feel about Jesus?**

Age Adjustments

FOR OLDER CHILDREN, plan a time to visit a local court of law. Observe as various people and attorneys argue their cases, and listen as the judge or jury determines appropriate punishments. Compare this process to God's judgment and forgiveness of us.

FOR YOUNGER CHILDREN, this activity is too difficult, and potentially frightening. Instead of setting up a court, remind your young child of something done wrong that same day. Together talk about how the child should be punished, then explain that you'll take the punishment for your child. For children of this age, make the punishment immediately tangible, like a spanking or having to stand in the corner for five minutes. After you're received the punishment, talk with your child about how Jesus took our punishment too, even though He hadn't done anything wrong.

Share: God loves us so much that even though we deserve to be punished by death, He sent Jesus to take the punishment for us. Even though we'll die someday, we'll be able to go to heaven and be with God. We won't be punished for all the sins we've done. Jesus took the punishment we deserve.

WRAP-UP

Gather everyone in a circle and have family members take turns answering this question: **What's one thing you've learned about God today?**

Next tell kids you've got a new "Life Slogan" you'd like to share with them.

Life Slogan: Today's Life Slogan is this, "When Jesus died that day, He took my sins away!" Have family members repeat the slogan two or three times to help them learn it. Then encourage them to practice saying it during the week so they can talk about it at your next family night session.

Close in Prayer: Allow time for each family member to share prayer concerns and answers to prayer. Then close your time together with prayer for each concern. Thank God for listening to and caring about us.

Remember to record your prayer requests so you can refer to them in the future as you see God answering them!

Additional Resources:

Baby Bible Stories about Jesus by Robin Currie (ages 1-4)
A First Look at Jesus by Lois Rock (ages 4-8)

© 3: Faith Is the Key

Exploring how faith in Jesus is the only way to God.

Scripture:
• Exodus 3:1-6—Moses and the Burning Bush.
• Mark 15:16-41—Jesus dies on the cross.
• John 14:6—Jesus is the only way to God.
• John 3:16—If we believe in Jesus, God will give us eternal life.
• Ephesians 2:8-9—We're saved by faith, not works.

ACTIVITY OVERVIEW		
Activity	Summary	Pre-Session Prep
Activity 1: Mr. Clean	Reach a clean area by walking through powder.	You'll need a roll of masking tape, a container of baby powder or corn starch, a broom, and a Bible.
Activity 2: A-Cross the Bridge	Construct a cross that also is a bridge.	You'll need a six-foot 2x4 piece of lumber and a three-foot 2x4, hammers, and nails.
Activity 3: Free Gift!	Trust a parent to provide a free gift later in the week.	You'll need an I.O.U. as described in the lesson for each family member.

Main Points:

— God is Holy.

— When Jesus took our punishment, He made a bridge for us to reach God.

— We reach God through faith in Jesus.

LIFE SLOGAN: "Jesus died for me, so with God I could be!"

Make it your own

In the space provided below, outline the flow and add any additional ideas to guide you through the process of conducting this family night.

Prayer & Praise Items

In the space provided below, list any items you wish to pray about or give praise for during this family night session.

Journal

In the space provided below, capture a record of any fun or meaningful things which happened during this family night session.

WARM-UP

Open with Prayer: Begin by having a family member pray, asking God to help everyone in the family understand more about Him through this time. After prayer, review your last lesson by asking these questions:

- **What's one thing you remember about our last lesson?**
- **Do you remember the Life Slogan?**
- **Have your actions changed because of what we learned? If so, how?** Encourage family members to give specific examples of how they've applied past learning.

Share: When Jesus died on the cross he took our punishment, but He also did something else! Today we're going to find out what that is!

ACTIVITY 1: Mr. Clean

Point: God is holy.

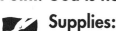 **Supplies:** You'll need a roll of masking tape and a container of baby powder or corn starch, a broom and a Bible.

Activity: Take your family outdoors to a large cemented or paved area. This could be your driveway, garage, a wide sidewalk, a ball court at a nearby park or other similar area.

If weather or lack of light requires your family to stay indoors, this activity can be done in an uncarpeted area such as the kitchen. Be sure to sweep up the powder after the activity, as vacuuming this much powder can cause clouds of dust!

Use masking tape to draw a square on the ground, large enough for a person to stand in. Then tape off a path, about three feet wide and five feet long, leading up to the square. Have family members help you liberally sprinkle powder or corn starch to completely cover the larger area, leaving the square clean.

When the larger are is filled in, have everyone gather at the end of the path farthest from the clean square and remove their shoes and socks.

Explain: **The goal of this activity is to walk across the powdered area in your bare feet, and step into the clean area without getting any of the powder in it.**

Let family members take turns walking, hopping, and tiptoeing toward the white area. No matter how carefully they walk, at least a tiny bit of powder will stick to their feet and come off in the clean area. Sweep the clean area after each turn so you can fairly judge the next family member's efforts.

When each person has had at least one turn, ask:

- **What do you think is the best technique for getting to the area with the least amount of powder on your feet?**
- **Is there any way to get to the clean square that we didn't try?** (*The impossibility of the task should be emphasized to set up the lesson of the activity.*)

Share: This activity reminds me of us and God. Let me read you a short story from the Bible to help explain what I mean.

 Read Exodus 3:1-6 aloud. Then discuss these questions:

- **Why did Moses have to take off his shoes?** (*They were too dirty to touch the holy ground.*)
- **What does it mean to be holy?** (*Separate; apart from anything unclean.*)
- **Why would Moses be afraid to even look at God?** (*God's power and perfection would seem overwhelming.*)
- **Does this story help you understand anything new about us and God?**

Share: To be holy means to be set apart, completely clean from sin. If the powder we used represented sin, the clean square at the end of the powdered path would be a holy area, but it would have to be even cleaner! There couldn't be even the tiniest speck of dust on that square!

God is holy. He's completely clean without even the *tiniest* speck of sin on Him. And just like our feet were covered with powder, our lives are covered with sin. That's why Moses couldn't even *look* at God. God is so holy, we can't even begin to get near Him!

Dust off all feet and have everyone put their shoes back on.

Share: Let's leave this powder here for a few minutes while we do our next activity. We'll come back to this later.

ACTIVITY 2: A-Cross the Bridge

Point: When Jesus took our punishment, He made a bridge for us to reach God.

 Supplies: You'll need a six-foot 2x4 piece of lumber, a three-foot 2x4, hammers, and nails.

Share: Jesus died on a cross to take the punishment for our sins. I thought we'd make a cross ourselves to help us think about what Jesus did.

Activity: Bring out the building supplies you've gathered. Place the six-foot length of 2x4 on the ground and place the three-foot length over it to form a cross. Have family members work together to hammer the nails through the center of the cross to keep it together. (The cross doesn't have to be perfect. It's more important for everyone to get a chance to help and enjoy working together.)

Age Adjustments

FOR YOUNGER CHILDREN, you may want to drill a few holes into the lumber ahead of time to make it easier for them to pound in the nails. Also, this activity may be too frightening for your child. Consider what you know of your child's ability to handle the thought of someone being beaten and nailed to a cross. If you choose to go ahead with the activity, be prepared to explain that it *was* terrible and cruel, but Jesus loved us enough to take this pain!

 As you work together, you might talk with your family about the pain Jesus must have felt as he was beaten and then nailed to a cross. If anyone accidentally hammers a finger or thumb, use that pain to make the moment even more teachable! (But do be careful!)

When the cross is finished, sit around it and **read** the biblical account of the crucifixion from Mark 15:16-41.

Ask family members to remain quiet for one minute and think about the pain and suffering Jesus went through as part of our punishment. After this minute, offer a short prayer of thanks to God for sending Jesus to take our punishment, and thank God for allowing Jesus to rise from the dead to prove His power over death!

Share: Jesus didn't deserve our punishment, but we're so thankful He took it! Now let me show you something else that Jesus' death did for us!

Activity: Carry the cross to the powdered area from the last activity. Place the longer beam over the length of powder.

Share: Now let's see who can get to the clean area without any powder on their feet!

Let family members take turns using the cross as a bridge over the powder and into the clean area.

Question:
- **How is the cross like a bridge?** *(It connects us with God, like a bridge joins two places.)*
- **How is Jesus' death like a bridge for us to reach God?** *(His sacrifice allows us to be made right, connected again with God.)*
- **Was it hard to stay on the bridge? How is that like staying out of sin in real life? How is it different?** *(While we can "slip up" and fall into sin, it happens by our choices, not by accident.)*

Share: Even though we made this cross and can use it to get to the clean area, we can never make a way to get to God. The Bible tells us this in John 14:6.

Read John 14:6 aloud and discuss:

- **What does this verse mean?** *(Jesus is the only way to God.)*
- **What are ways people try to get to God?** *(By doing good deeds, giving money to the church, being "good.")* **Why won't these ways work?** *(No one can ever be perfect; no deed is good enough.)*

Share: There are people who think they can work hard enough and be good enough to get to God. But no matter how hard we try to be good, we will always have at least a little sin in our lives. We didn't deserve it, but God gave us Jesus as a free gift!

ACTIVITY 3: Free Gift!

Point: We reach God through our faith in Jesus.

Supplies: You'll need an I.O.U. for each family member. Make these like coupons, owing each family member something different. For example, "This coupon good for breakfast with Dad at (name of restaurant) on Tuesday morning." Or, "Mom will meet you for an hour of window shopping after school on Friday." Other ideas could be a movie date, an evening making brownies with a parent, meeting your child at school for lunch, and so on. Think of the different interests of your family members as you create the I.O.U.'s. Place each coupon in an envelope with the appropriate family member's name on it.

Share: I want to give each of you a special gift. It's not something I have with me right now, so I'll give you an I.O.U. That means I'll owe you this gift later this week. You'll have to trust me that I really will give you your gift!

I'm giving you these gifts because I love you. You didn't earn the gift, and even if you do something wrong, I won't take this gift away.

Give each person his or her I.O.U. and allow these to be opened and read.

Ask:

- **How do you know I'll follow through and give you what your coupon says?**
- **How do you feel about waiting for your gift, and having to trust that I'll actually give it to you?**

Read John 3:16 and Ephesians 2:8-9 together then discuss:

- **What kind of gift is God giving us?** *(The gift of eternal life.)*
- **How do we get the gift?** *(Faith; Believing God really will give us this gift because Jesus died for us.)*
- **How is this like the gift I've given you?** *(We have to trust Jesus to give it to us.)*

Share: When you trust that I'll give you your gift later this week, you have faith in me. And when you have faith in Jesus, you trust that He's taken your punishment and made a way for you to reach God. God is holy, and the only way to reach Him is through faith in Jesus.

Special Note To Parents—Be sure you follow through with the gift you've promised! During the promised time you spend with your child, talk more about how your child's trust in you is like our trust in Jesus.

WRAP-UP

Gather everyone in a circle and have family members take turns answering this question: **What's one thing you've learned about God today?**

Next tell kids you've got a new "Life Slogan" you'd like to share with them.

Life Slogan: Today's Life Slogan is this, "Jesus died for me so with God I could be." Have family members repeat the slogan two or three times to help them learn it. Then encourage them to practice saying it during the week so they can talk about it at your next family night session.

Close in Prayer: Allow time for each family member to share prayer concerns and answers to prayer. Then close your time together with prayer for each concern. Thank God for listening to and caring about us.

Remember to record your prayer requests so you can refer to them in the future as you see God answering them!

Additional Resources:

The King Without a Shadow by R.C. Sproul (family reading)
Let's Talk About Heaven by Debby Anderson (ages 4-8)
Lassie to the Rescue adapted by Marian Bray (ages 8-12)

☺ 4: Who's in Charge Here?

Exploring the role of the Holy Spirit in our lives.

Scripture:
- John 14:23-26—God will send the Holy Spirit.
- 1 Corinthians 2:12—The Holy Spirit helps us understand God's gift of salvation.
- Galatians 5:19-26—The acts of a sinful nature and the fruits of the Spirit.

ACTIVITY OVERVIEW		
Activity	Summary	Pre-Session Prep
Activity 1: Power Supply	Compare a flashlight and batteries to us and the Holy Spirit.	You'll need flashlights with batteries, candy or other small treats, and a Bible. Hide treats as discussed in lesson.
Activity 2: Listen Closely	Listen to a guiding voice for direction.	You'll need blindfolds.
Activity 3: Turn On the Holy Spirit!	Place reminders to choose to listen to the Holy Spirit around the home.	You'll need 3x5 cards or paper, markers, and tape.

Main Points:

— The Holy Spirit lives in us if we believe in Jesus Christ as our Saviour.

— We must listen to hear the Holy Spirit.

— We must choose to obey.

LIFE SLOGAN: "If obeying God is your goal, then give His Spirit full-control!"

Make it your own

In the space provided below, outline the flow and add any additional ideas to guide you through the process of conducting this family night.

Prayer & Praise Items

In the space provided below, list any items you wish to pray about or give praise for during this family night session.

Journal

In the space provided below, capture a record of any fun or meaningful things which happened during this family night session.

WARM-UP

Open with Prayer: Begin by having a family member pray, asking God to help everyone in the family understand more about Him through this time. After prayer, review your last lesson by asking these questions:

- **What activity do you remember from our last lesson? What special meaning did that activity have?**
- **Do you remember the Life Slogan?**
- **Have your actions changed because of what we learned? If so, how?** Encourage family members to give specific examples of how they've applied past learning.

ACTIVITY 1: Power Supply

Point: The Holy Spirit lives in those who believe in Jesus Christ as Savior.

Supplies: You'll need a flashlight for each family member, candy or fruit or other small treats such as stickers or crayons, and a Bible.

Activity: Before you gather your family, hide the candy or other treats in your home. Let the ages of your children determine how well the candy is hidden, choosing obvious hiding places for younger children and more challenging places for older children.

Share: I've hidden treats for you around the house. Here are some flashlights to use to find them!

Give each child a flashlight and turn off the lights or close the curtains to darken your home.

Give everyone plenty of time to hunt with their flashlights. When everything has been found, gather everyone together and turn the lights back on.

Question:
- **What made this game hard for you? What made it easier?**
- **What kind of help did your flashlight give you?**

Share: Our flashlights can help us to learn about the Holy Spirit. Let's read a few verses from the Bible, then talk more about our flashlights and the Holy Spirit.

 Read John 14:23-26 and 1 Corinthians 2:12 together.

Share: These verses tell us that when Jesus went back to Heaven to live, God sent the Holy Spirit. From these verses what do we know about the Holy Spirit? (God will send the Holy Spirit. The Holy Spirit helps us understand salvation).

Share: The Holy Spirit does many things. These verses tell us that the Holy Spirit teaches us, reminds us of what Jesus said, and helps us understand the free gift of salvation.

I can think of three ways our flashlights can help us understand the Holy Spirit. I'll give you a clue for each way!

Clue 1: Light.
Clue 2: Power.
Clue 3: On/off switch.

Give each of these clues and wait a minute or two for family members to share their thoughts regarding the Holy Spirit's connection to this clue. After everyone has had a chance to share, explain what you meant by the clue.

Clue 1: Light: When we believe in Jesus as our Savior, He sends the Holy Spirit to help us find our way through life, just like the light of the flashlight helped you find your treats.

Clue 2: Power: Our flashlights get their power from batteries. (Open a flashlight and take out the batteries for everyone to look at.) **The Holy Spirit in us is like the batteries in the flashlight. They're always there to give power to the flashlight, just like the Holy Spirit is always there to give us the power to do what God wants us to do.**

Clue 3: On/Off Switch: The on/off switch on the flashlight tells the flashlight to use the power of the batteries or not to use the power. In our lives this is our will. We can decide to let the Holy Spirit

Age Adjustments

FOR OLDER CHILDREN, use a remote controlled car. Have children drive the car through an obstacle course they've created. Then discuss these questions:

- How are the obstacles here like ones we face in life?
- How are we like the car?
- How is God like the remote control?
- How are the batteries like the Holy Spirit?

Use the verses from the flashlight activity as well as Romans 8:8-11 in your discussion.

use His power to help us do things God's way, or we can choose to do things our own way.

? **Question: When we sin, is the power switch in our lives on or off?** *(We are turning off the power switch of the Spirit when we go our own way.)*

ACTIVITY 2: Listen Closely

Point: We must listen to hear the Holy Spirit.

 Supplies: You'll need blindfolds.

Activity: Ask for one child to volunteer to be blindfolded. Carefully cover this child's eyes so he or she cannot see. Explain that you'll be using your voice to direct this child into another room of the house. While you're talking, have the other family members call out wrong directions to try and confuse the blindfolded child.

After the first child has either successfully completed the mission, or given up, let other family members try being blindfolded and repeat the activity. Choose different areas of your home to direct each person to, with one person giving the correct directions while everyone else shouts the wrong ones. Be sure to try this yourself, choosing one of the children to give you directions while you're blindfolded.

When everyone has had a turn, discuss these questions:
- **How did you feel when you were blindfolded?** *(Confused, lost.)*
- **What made moving about the house easier or harder for you?** *(probably the others shouting wrong directions.)*
- **Was it easy to hear the correct guiding voice?**
- **How is this activity like listening to the Holy Spirit?** *(His voice can help us find our way.)*

• What "voices" in real life keep you from listening to the Holy Spirit? *(Our wants, desires, or temptations.)*
• How do you know if you're listening to the Holy Spirit or not?

Share: When we decide not to listen to the Holy Spirit we often choose our own selfish and wrong ways. We decide not to listen to God, but to listen to ideas telling us to do wrong. In order to do what is best, we have to listen to the Holy Spirit. The Bible gives us some examples of how we can tell if we're listening to God or ignoring Him.

 Read Galatians 5:19-26 aloud.

Question:
• **Do any of these acts of the sinful nature remind you of things you've done?** *(Be sure family members share only what they want to tell. Don't let this become a time of tattling on the sins of others!)*

Age Adjustments

YOUNGER CHILDREN **may be frightened by being blindfolded. If you think this might upset your child, only cover the eyes of your older children.**

Another way to help a younger child understand the Holy Spirit is to compare the Holy Spirit to a blanket or stuffed animal that brings comfort and peace.

Take several minutes to affirm each family member by completing this sentence: **I see this fruit of the Spirit (name one) in (family member) when (give example).** For example, "I see the fruit of the Spirit of gentleness in Annette. I noticed earlier this week she found a hurt bird and Annette was so careful and gentle as she wrapped it up and fed it." Or "I see the fruit of the Spirit of self-control in Joel. Yesterday some of his friends were trying to get him to watch an R-rated movie. But Joel controlled himself and come home instead of doing what was wrong."

Be sure to affirm each family member at least once. If you like, encourage others to point out ways they've also seen family members display fruits of the Spirit.

ACTIVITY 3: Turn On the Power!

Point: We must choose to obey.

 Supplies: You'll need 3x5 cards or slips of paper, markers and tape.

Share: We have the Holy Spirit in our lives, but we have to remember to turn the power switch on to the Holy Spirit and listen to Him instead of turning it off and ignoring Him. I know a way we can remind ourselves to do this in the next week.

Activity: Have family members write the following phrase on the different cards or slips of paper: Turn on the Power. Turn on (name a specific fruit of the Spirit). For example, "Turn on the Power. Turn on love!" Make at least one paper for each of the fruit of the Spirit.

Then walk around the house together and tape these papers below or near various power switches in your home. You might place one under each bedroom light switch, another beside the outlet where a daughter plugs in her curling iron, and another near the ignition of the car.

As you tape each paper into place, think together of specific ways family members can demonstrate the various fruits during the week. For example, as you tape "Turn on patience" in your car, family members might think of being patient in traffic, being patient while waiting for your turn, or being patient when you think someone has misunderstood what you're saying.

Then return to your original meeting area for Wrap-Up.

WRAP-UP

Gather everyone in a circle and have family members take turns answering this question: **What's one thing you've learned about God today?**

Next tell kids you've got a new "Life Slogan" you'd like to share with them.

Life Slogan: Today's Life Slogan is this, "If obeying God is your goal, then give His Spirit full-control!" Have family members repeat the slogan two or three times to help them learn it. Then encourage them to practice saying it during the week so they can talk about it at your next family night session.

Close in Prayer: Allow time for each family member to share prayer concerns and answers to prayer. Then close your time together with prayer for each concern. Thank God for listening to and caring about us.

Remember to record your prayer requests so you can refer to them in the future as you see God answering them!

Additional Resources

My First Prayers by Debby Anderson (ages 1-4)
God Can Do Anything by Mary Erickson (ages 4-8)
From Paul With Love by Peter Rogers (ages 6-11)

⊙ 5: Love That Can't Sit Still

Exploring service as an expression of love.

Scripture:
• Galatians 5:13—Serve one another in love.
• Hebrews 13:1-3—We can show love by helping those in need.
• Colossians 3:23-24—It is Christ we are truly serving.

ACTIVITY OVERVIEW		
Activity	Summary	Pre-Session Prep
Activity 1: Mine, All Mine	Determine the meaning of selfishness.	You'll need a bag of candy and a Bible.
Activity 2: Penny Auction	Plan a family service project.	none
Activity 3: Secret Service of Love	Serve Jesus by serving each other.	You'll need paper, scissors, and pens.

Main Points:

—Acting selfishly is the opposite of being loving and serving.

—Our family can show love by serving others.

—We can show love by serving family members.

LIFE SLOGAN: "When my love is true, actions show it to you!"

Make it your own

In the space provided below, outline the flow and add any additional ideas to guide you through the process of conducting this family night.

Prayer & Praise Items

In the space provided below, list any items you wish to pray about or give praise for during this family night session.

Journal

In the space provided below, capture a record of any fun or meaningful things which happened during this family night session.

WARM-UP

Open with Prayer: Begin by having a family member pray, asking God to help everyone in the family understand more about Him through this time. After prayer, review your last lesson by asking these questions:

- **What did we learn about in our last lesson?**
- **Do you remember the Life Slogan?**
- **Have your actions changed because of what we learned? If so, how?** Encourage family members to give specific examples of how they've applied past learning.

Share: Today we'll be learning about one of the fruits of the Spirit— Love.

ACTIVITY 1: Mine, All Mine

Point: Acting selfishly is the opposite of being loving and serving.

Supplies: You'll need a bag of small candies, with at least three pieces per child.

Activity: Empty the bag of candy in the center of your family circle and tell kids they can take as many pieces as they like. Wait to see how children determine who gets how much candy. Don't interfere as they divide the loot.

When the candy is divided, whether fairly or not, discuss:

- **When I said you could have as much as you wanted, what did you think? What did you do?**
- **Do you think you were selfish?**
- **How do your actions prove whether or not you're selfish?**
- **What do you think it means to be selfish?** (*Wanting to keep things to yourself, not sharing.*)
- **What do you think is the opposite of being selfish?** (*Being generous; being loving.*)

Adjustments for an only child

If you have only one child in your family, see if the child keeps all the candy, or shares any with you. Ask the child what he or she plans to do with the candy. Perhaps your child will want to share it with friends, save it, or eat it all at once.

Read Galatians 5:13 together, then ask:

- **What do you think the Bible means when it says not to "indulge the sinful nature"?** *(Don't do what comes naturally—being selfish.)*
- **How is showing your love by serving others the opposite of being selfish?** *(You put others first.)*
- **How has Jesus unselfishly shown us His love?** *(He came to earth and died on the cross for us.)*

Age Adjustments

FOR OLDER CHILDREN, you might use quarters or dollar bills instead of candy in this activity.

If you're concerned about your children eating too much candy, use other small treats they would enjoy for this activity. Consider new pencils, stickers, or small toys instead of candy.

Share: When we're selfish we're only thinking of ourselves. When we love others, we think of them first, and want to serve them.

ACTIVITY 2: Penny Auction

Point: Our family can show love by serving others.

Share: Here's a true story about some people who thought of others before themselves.

Activity: Read the following story aloud.

A dime for a horse! A quarter for a tractor! A cow for only three cents!

Can you imagine shopping at prices like these? The people who paid these prices weren't really shopping. They were helping their friends. Let me explain.

In the 1930's the United States went through a time called the Great Depression. During this time many factories, banks and stores closed. Millions of people lost their jobs, all their money, and their homes.

Also during this time, the middle areas of the United States such as Kansas, Oklahoma, and Colorado, were without rain for a long time, and the land became very dry. Huge windstorms blew the dusty soil away. Can you imagine what this might have been like?

With no rain and so much wind, most farmers couldn't grow anything on their land. They became poorer and poorer, and often borrowed money from the bank for things they needed. But when the farmers couldn't pay back the money they owed, the banks would come and auction off everything the farmer and his family owned. This was sort of like a garage sale, but *everything* had to be sold to satisfy the bank. How would you feel if you were in this situation?

Well the farmers cared about each other, and figured out a way to help each other during these hard times. When a bank would come to sell everything a farmer had, his friends would only bid a pennies on what was for sale. That's how they'd get a horse for only a dime, or a tractor for twenty-five cents. The bank never made much money on these "penny auctions," but what could they do? They'd sold everything the farmer had!

Then later, the friends would come and give the farmer back everything they'd bought from him! Instead of thinking how lucky they were to buy a horse for ten cents, they gave it up for their friend!

Discuss:

- **How do you think the farmers and their families felt about selling all their things?** (unhappy.)
- **How do you think they felt when their friends gave everything back to them?** (surprised, happy, thankful.)
- **How were the people who bought the items back for their friends not being selfish?** (They spent their money to help others.)
- **There aren't penny auctions anymore, so how can we show love to others like this today?** (Brainstorm ideas for helping others.)

 Read Hebrews 13:1-3, as a Biblical discussion of how to love.

Question:

- **Who do you know that needs to be shown love?**
- **Why are our actions so important in showing love?** (Actions often speak louder than words.)

Age Adjustments

FOR SCHOOL-AGED CHILDREN AND YOUNGER, check your library or bookstore for *Leah's Pony* (Boyds Mills Press) by Elizabeth Friedrich. This wonderful story of a young farm girl whose family loses everything during the Depression captures the drama and feeling of a penny auction.

IF YOU HAVE OLDER CHILDREN, plan an evening to volunteer together at a soup kitchen, homeless shelter or other service agency. You may find yourself sorting canned food or mending donated clothing together as you serve God in love! An additional Bible passage for discussion before this activity is 1 John 3:16-17.

Depending on the laws in your area, teenagers may be able to visit prisons. See what kind of Bible studies or services are held at the nearest jail or prison and find out how your family can volunteer.

Activity: As a family, think of an unselfish way you can show love to another person or family in need. For example, you might take a few blankets to a homeless shelter, do yard work for an elderly neighbor, or take a meal to a family in need. Plan this project now, deciding who to help, and exactly when you all will carry out the plan.

ACTIVITY 3: Secret Service of Love

Point: We can show love by serving family members.

 Supplies: You'll need paper, scissors and pens.

Share: It's great that we're able to serve. We don't even have to leave our homes to show love by serving. We can serve each other!

Activity: Have each family member, including yourself, draw and cut out seven hearts, about three or four inches in size. (Younger children may need help with drawing and cutting.) On each of their hearts, have the family member write, "Secret Service of Love." If you like, provide sticker, crayons or markers so each person can personalize their hearts.

Share: During the next week we can secretly show our love to other family members with these hearts. Every day, think of one way to serve another family member and secretly do it. Then leave one of your hearts at that spot as a further reminder of your love!

 Read Colossians 3:23-24 aloud.

Question:
- **What does this verse mean?** *(When we help others, we are really serving Jesus.)*
- **How should we go about our secret service mission this week?** *(Let everyone suggest some ideas.)*
- **Whom are we really serving with our actions?** *(Jesus.)*
- **How does knowing you're serving Jesus make you feel about serving?**

Together brainstorm ways to serve other family members. If you like, make a list to post on the refrigerator to spark ideas later in the week. Your list might include taking the trash out, making someone's bed, vacuuming, feeding or walking the dog, driving someone to school, packing a lunch, and other similar ideas.

WRAP-UP

Gather everyone in a circle and have family members take turns answering this question: What's one thing you've learned about God today?

Next tell kids you've got a new "Life Slogan" you'd like to share with them.

Life Slogan: Today's Life Slogan is this, "When my love is true, actions show it to you!" Have family members repeat the slogan two or three times to help them learn it. Then encourage them to practice saying it during the week so they can talk about it at your next family night session.

> ## Age Adjustments
>
> FOR OLDER CHILDREN, further your discussion of what the Bible teaches on showing love through actions by reading 1 John 3:11-20. Discuss these questions:
> - What do these verses mean?
> - Why are our thoughts and actions both important?
> - What do you think verse 18 means?
> - How do these verses apply to your life?

Close in Prayer: Allow time for each family member to share prayer concerns and answers to prayer. Then close your time together with prayer for each concern. Thank God for listening to and caring about us.

Remember to record your prayer requests so you can refer to them in the future as you see God answering them!

Additional Resources:

The Toddlers Bedtime Story Book by V. Gilbert Beers (ages 1-3)
Jesus Loves Me by Debby Anderson (ages 1-4)
Rattlebang by Mark McCord (ages 4-7)

6: "Obey" Isn't *Really* a Four-Letter Word

Exploring obedience to God and authorities

Scripture:
• Exodus 20:12—Honor your parents.
• Joshua 1:16-18 and 6:1-21—Joshua and the battle of Jericho.

ACTIVITY OVERVIEW		
Activity	Summary	Pre-Session Prep
Activity 1: Umbrella of Obedience	Discover the reason for rules.	You'll need paper, pencil, candy, an umbrella, soft objects, masking tape, a pen and a Bible.
Activity 2: Read the directions.	See a final picture as a result of obedience.	You'll need pencil and paper.
Activity 3: Map it Out!	Follow directions to a surprise destination.	You'll need 3x5 cards.

Main Points:
—We're protected through obedience.
—To know God's plans we must obey.
—Obedience has good rewards.

LIFE SLOGAN: "When we obey, we go the right way!"

Make it your own
In the space provided below, outline the flow and add any additional ideas to guide you through the process of conducting this family night.

Prayer & Praise Items
In the space provided below, list any items you wish to pray about or give praise for during this family night session.

Journal
In the space provided below, capture a record of any fun or meaningful things which happened during this family night session.

WARM-UP

Open with Prayer: Begin by having a family member pray, asking God to help everyone in the family understand more about Him through this time. After prayer, review your last lesson by asking these questions:

• **What do you remember from our last lesson?**

• **Do you remember the Life Slogan?**

• **Have your actions changed because of what we learned? If so, how?** Encourage family members to give specific examples of how they've applied past learning.

Share: Another way we show our love to God is by obeying Him. Today we're going to discover why obedience is important.

ACTIVITY 1: Umbrella of Obedience

Point: We're protected through obedience.

Supplies: You'll need paper and pencil, small candies or other small treats, one or more umbrellas (you'll need one for every 2-3 family members), soft objects from around your house such as stuffed animals, bean bags, or even balled-up socks, masking tape, a pen and a Bible.

Activity: Make a list of rules your family lives under. Together brainstorm different rules from your home, schools, and work. Include basic laws of the land as well. Make a list down one side of your paper. Your list might include, don't answer the door if a parent isn't home, look both ways before crossing the street, no hitting or name-calling, drive within the speed limits, and so on. Stop when you have 10-12 rules.

Discuss what could happen if you break these rules. Write down the negative results beside the corresponding rule. For example, next to "look both ways before crossing the street," you could write, "get hit by a car." Next to "no hitting" you might write "no dessert," or whatever your family punishment would be.

When you've completed the list of rules and their consequences, bring out the umbrellas.

Share: When we obey rules, it's like being under an umbrella of protection.

Activity continued: Take a piece of the masking tape and tape it onto the umbrella. Write OBEY on this tape. (If you're using more than one umbrella, tape OBEY on all of them.) Then have family members help you place tape on the soft objects you've gathered. On the tape, write different consequences for breaking rules from your list. For example, on the tape of one object you might write "get a speeding ticket," and on another write "no dessert."

Gather the soft objects into a pile beside you. Have all other family members go about five feet away from you and hide behind the open umbrella. Place the candy or other treats beside you.

Say: If you come out from behind the umbrella you can get some of the candy!

Continue to tempt family members in this way until one of them gives in and comes out from behind the umbrella. Throw one or more of the soft objects at the family member saying, "Ben just got hit by a car!" or "No dessert this week for Kelly!" according to what was written on the soft object. Don't let the child have the candy either.

Keep on taunting and tempting family members until you've hit them all with a soft object or until you're sure no one else will venture out from behind the umbrella. Then put the umbrella and candy away.

Discuss:
- **Why do we have rules?** *(They keep us safe.)*
- **What rule is hardest for you to obey and why?** *(Let each person share.)*
- **Are some rules more important than others? If so, what ones? If not, why are all rules important?**
- **What rules does God have for us?** *(Name rules from the Bible that help us.)*
- **Why is it important to obey God?** *(When we don't, it hurts us because we have to deal with the consequences.)*

Note: If any of your family members tried to get to the candy by moving the umbrella, discuss how people try to "bend" rules. Is bending a rule breaking a rule? Why or why not?

Share: Most rules are for our protection. God gave ten rules to his people a long time ago. We call those rules The Ten Commandments. Let's read one of those now.

 Read Exodus 20:12 then ask:

- **How is obeying our parents a way of honoring them?** (*It shows we love and respect them.*)
- **Why do you think God made this one of his commandments, right up there with telling us not to kill?** (*It starts us out right in life.*)
- **How do you think honoring and obeying your parents will help you to "live long"?** (*We make better choices, which can lead to happier, healthier lives.*)

> ## Age Adjustments
>
> YOUNGER CHILDREN may further understand this activity if you draw a simple picture of your family standing beneath an umbrella with rain falling around. Make the comparison that just as the umbrella keeps off rain, obedience keeps away harm.

Share: Obeying rules often protects us and others from danger. When we obey our parents, teachers, employers, and others in authority, it often is for our own safety and protection.

ACTIVITY 2: Read the Directions

Point: To know God's plans we must obey.

 Supplies: You'll need paper and pencil. Before your family time, draw dots on several sheets of paper that, when properly connected, will create a star. Number the dots on some papers, leaving others without numbers.

Activity: Give each person a dot-to-dot paper you've prepared and a pencil. Be sure family members don't let others see their papers.

Share: Without looking at anyone else's paper, connect these dots to make a picture.

When each person is finished, look and see that each person has created.

Discuss:
- **How did following the numbers help?**
- **If you didn't have numbers, how did you feel while doing this activity?**

- How is following the numbers like obeying?
- We were able to create a star by obeying the directions. What does God create in us when we obey Him?

Share: When we obey God, He's able to use us for His purposes. A story in the Bible demonstrates this. In the Old Testament, Moses was a great leader of the Israelites. When he died, God told Joshua to become the next leader.

Read Joshua 1:16-18.

Share: The people did obey Joshua, even when situations seemed dangerous or the directions seemed strange. One time God gave instructions to Joshua that seemed very strange, but Joshua and the people he was leading followed the directions.

Read Joshua 6:1-21, then discuss:

- **How do you think Joshua and his followers felt marching around and around the city of their enemies day after day?** *(Perhaps some felt foolish while others trusted God.)*
- **What happened because they did obey?** *(They won an "impossible" battle.)*
- **Do you ever feel foolish or uncomfortable about obeying the rules or directions of our family? What about at school, in sports, or in other situations?**
- **How does obeying the directions of your parents, teachers, or coaches bring a good outcome?** *(Encourage all to give examples.)*

Age Adjustments

FOR YOUNGER CHILDREN, paraphrase the story of Joshua and the battle of Jericho, or read the story from a good children's Bible-story book.

FOR CHILDREN OF ALL AGES, try this. If your budget permits, purchase several dot-to-dot books and cover the numbers with correction fluid. See how many pictures family members can correctly complete without the directions!

FOR OLDER CHILDREN, purchase a model car or other item that requires directions. See how well family members can get along without directions, then read the directions to see how much easier the object is to assemble.

Share: When we drew the dot-to-dots, the outcome of the picture wasn't clear. When Joshua and his followers obeyed God, they didn't know until the last day what the result would be. And when we obey God, we don't know where He'll lead us or what He'll ask us to do, but we know it will be for good in the end.

ACTIVITY 3: Map it Out!

Point: Obedience has good rewards.

 Supplies: Before your family time, plan an outing all family members will enjoy. This might be a trip to an ice cream shop, a visit with favorite friends, an outing to the movies, a stop at a local park, or something of this nature. Write specific directions to this location on several 3x5 cards, not giving away your destination until the last card. Number the cards in their correct order. For example, card one might say, "Start car, place it in reverse and back out of the driveway. Go left until the first stop sign, then pull over and read card two." Place these cards in an envelope.

Activity: Have everyone pile into the car for a surprise outing. Give one child the envelope. Announce that (name of child with the envelope) is in charge and that you will drive according to the directions she gives.

As your child reads the first card, do everything possible to not obey the directions. Turn in the wrong direction, pull into gas stations or other drive-ways, and so on. If family members complain use responses like, "I think I know better than Bobby (or whatever child's name is) how to get where we're going!" or "I think this way will get us there too," or other similar answers. Let different family members try giving you the directions, but always disobey.

When you've finally ended up at a farm, Laundromat or some other destination you *really don't* want to be at, say: **I've blown it. I didn't obey the directions, and now we're at the wrong place. Let's go home and try again.**

When you get home, sort the cards into the correct order again, and this time, do follow the directions. As you drive, talk about how God leads us, how frustrating life can be when we don't obey, and other consequences of disobedience. When

Age Adjustments

FOR YOUNGER CHILDREN **that don't yet read, give the directions to another adult in your family, or read them aloud yourself, making sure the children know you're not following the directions you just read.**

FOR OLDER CHILDREN, **try plotting out directions to your location on a map. Let them give you directions in the same manner, only following the plan on a map.**

you've arrived at your fun location, enjoy you time together celebrating the joy of obedience!

WRAP-UP

Gather everyone in a circle and have family members take turns answering this question: What's one thing you've learned about God today?

Next tell kids you've got a new "Life Slogan" you'd like to share with them.

Life Slogan: Today's Life Slogan is this, "When we obey, we go the right way!" Have family members repeat the slogan two or three times to help them learn it. Then encourage them to practice saying it during the week so they can talk about it at your next family night session.

Close in Prayer: Allow time for each family member to share prayer concerns and answers to prayer. Then close your time together with prayer for each concern. Thank God for listening to and caring about us.

Remember to record your prayer requests so you can refer to them in the future as you see God answering them!

Additional Resources

Rainy Day Rescue by Barbara Davoll (ages 4-8)
Adam Raccoon in Lost Woods by Glen Keane (ages 4-8)
Sarah's Journey: Reunion in Kentucky by Wanda Lutrell (ages 8-12)

7: With All Due Respect

Exploring the power of respectful attitudes

Scripture:
- John 13:1-17—Jesus washes his follower's feet.
- Ephesians 6:1-8—Respect family members and employers.
- 1 Peter 2:13-17—Respect those in authority.
- Psalm 119:17—Respect God's word.
- James 2:1-12—Don't give respect based on material wealth.
- 1 Timothy 4:12—How to earn respect.

ACTIVITY OVERVIEW

Activity	Summary	Pre-Session Prep
Activity 1: Rinsing on Respect	Wash feet of family members.	You'll need a basin of warm water, towels and a Bible.
Activity 2: Who and How	Determine who God wants us to respect and how to do this.	You'll need paper, pen, and tape.
Activity 3: Show Some Respect!	We can respect each other.	none

Main Points:

— We can show respect by serving.

— The Bible tells us who we should respect.

— We can show love through respecting family members.

LIFE SLOGAN: "Respond with Respect!"

Make it your own
In the space provided below, outline the flow and add any additional ideas to guide you through the process of conducting this family night.

Prayer & Praise Items
In the space provided below, list any items you wish to pray about or give praise for during this family night session.

Journal
In the space provided below, capture a record of any fun or meaningful things which happened during this family night session.

WARM-UP

Open with Prayer: Begin by having a family member pray, asking God to help everyone in the family understand more about Him through this time. After prayer, review your last lesson by asking these questions:

- **What do you remember from our last lesson?**
- **Do you remember the Life Slogan?**
- **Have your actions changed because of what we learned? If so, how?** Encourage family members to give specific examples of how they've applied past learning.

Share: When we obey God and those He's made leaders over us, we're showing respect. Tonight we're going to learn more about what it means to show respect to others.

ACTIVITY 1: Rinsing with Respect

Point: We can show respect by serving.

Supplies: You'll need a bucket or basin of warm, soapy water, towels and a Bible.

Have family members sit in a circle.

Share: In Bible times, everyone wore sandals. They didn't have sidewalks and paved roads like we do. They walked on dusty paths. This meant their feet got very dirty in their sandals. Whenever a guest would come into your home, one of your servants would wash the guest's feet. This showed you respected your guest and cared about his or her comfort. Even though this is an old-fashioned practice, I'd like us to try it now in our family.

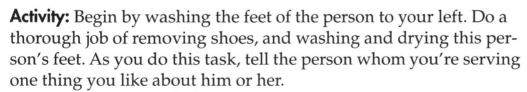

Activity: Begin by washing the feet of the person to your left. Do a thorough job of removing shoes, and washing and drying this person's feet. As you do this task, tell the person whom you're serving one thing you like about him or her.

When you've completed the washing, have the person with the clean feet wash the next person's feet in the same manner. Ask family members to share something they like about the person whose feet they're washing. If necessary, remind them to refrain from complaining or making negative comments about the smell of other's feet. This is a time of respect, not of cutting down.

 When the last person has washed your feet, **read** John 13:1-17 aloud and question:

- **Why did Jesus wash the feet of his followers?** (*To demonstrate His role as a servant.*)
- **What did they think about Jesus washing their feet?** (*Peter didn't want Him to at first, but he changed his mind when he realized Jesus truly wanted to serve him.*)
- **What did you think about our washing feet together?** (*Let all share.*)
- **How did you feel about washing or having your feet washed?**
- **What does it mean to show respect to others?** (*We put their needs ahead of our own.*)
- **Why is washing feet a way of showing respect?** (*It has one person serving, humbly.*)
- **How do you normally like people to show respect for you?**
- **How do you show respect to others?**

ACTIVITY 2: Who and How

Point: The Bible tells us who we should respect.

 Supplies: You'll need a large sheet of paper, tape, a pen and a Bible.

Activity: Form two columns on the paper, labeling one "Who" and the other "How." Tape this paper to a wall or window where it can be seen by everyone. Tell the family you are each going to read verses in the Bible that tell us who we should respect and how we should do it. Have family members take turns reading the passages. After each reading, fill in the columns of who or what the Bible is talking about, and specific ways the Bible says to show respect.

 Read:
- **Ephesians 6:1-8**—Children show respect by obeying parents; Fathers respect children by teaching them about the Lord; Slaves respect masters by obeying them.
- **1 Peter 2:13-17**—People show respect to the government by obeying laws.

• **Psalm 119:17**—We respect God by obeying His Word.

 Question:

• **What do these verses and our study of them teach you about respect?** (*Respect is based on putting others first.*)
• **Are there others who should be on this list as well? If so, add them.** (*Give time to brainstorm ideas.*)
• **What are other ways to show respect for these people?** (*Let everyone share.*)

Share: The Bible also tells gives us information on how to decide whom to respect.

 Read James 2:1-12 and discuss:

• **Should we respect someone more or less because of the amount of money they have?** (*Money should make no difference.*) **Why or why not?** (*It is wrong to judge outward appearances.*)
• **What about someone who has a lot of nice clothes, cars or other things—should we give them more respect than someone who is poor or dresses in old clothes? Why or why not?** (*It is wrong because the heart and actions speak louder than clothes and possessions.*)
• **How can you decide who deserves to be shown respect?** (*You need to listen and observe, so you can learn from those who are following God's Word.*)

Age Adjustments

FOR YOUNGER CHILDREN, focus only on the Ephesians passage. In your discussion, include specific and practical ways to show respect such as following simple table manners, listening with others are talking, or not interrupting conversations.

HAVE OLDER CHILDREN, look through recent news magazines and find articles relating to showing respect for others. Some people demand respect through force, such as dictators or even armed gang members. Others earn it through their actions, such as Mother Theresa. When the children have found several articles, read them together and talk about the best ways to earn respect.

Share: God wants us to be respectful of everyone, especially those in authority, our family, and other Christians.

 Read 1 Timothy 4:12 and discuss how it says we can earn the respect of others. (Set an example in uprights speech, life, love, faith, and purity.)

If you are doing the next activity:

Share: Now that we know who we should respect and how to earn respect, let's see about putting respect into action.

ACTIVITY 3: Show Some Respect!

Point: We can show love through respecting family members.

 Supplies: You'll need paper and pencil.

Share: Let's list ways to show respect to others in our family, as well as listing how we like to be shown respect.

Activity: Give each family member a chance to share ways others can show respect to him or her, listing these as they're said. These might include, knocking on the bedroom door before entering, not teasing a child about a boyfriend or girlfriend, not whining about what's for dinner that night, and so on. You might also include a section at the end of the list including ways to demonstrate respect for all family members. These could be actions such as not inter-rupting conversations, being quiet when others are on the phone or doing homework, remembering to say "please" and "thank you," and so on.

When the list is complete, read it aloud again to help others remember. Suggest that each person choose three things to work on during the week, since it would be hard to remember all of them.

Have family members tell which actions they'll work hard at remembering, being sure each family member has one or two items of respect chosen. If it will help everyone remem-ber better, post the list on the refrigerator or on the bathroom wall as a reminder of how to show respect.

Age Adjustments

FOR YOUNGER CHILDREN, focus on one respectful action that the entire family will work on for the week. It's impor-tant that you show this same respect to your children as they show you.

WRAP-UP

Gather everyone in a circle and have family members take turns answering this question: **What's one thing you've learned about God today?**

Next tell kids you've got a new "Life Slogan" you'd like to share with them.

Life Slogan: Today's Life Slogan is this: "Respond with Respect!" Have family members repeat the slogan two or three times to help them learn it. Then encourage them to practice saying it during the week so they can talk about it at your next family night session.

Close in Prayer: Allow time for each family member to share prayer concerns and answers to prayer. Then close your time together with prayer for each concern. Thank God for listening to and caring about us.

Remember to record your prayer requests so you can refer to them in the future as you see God answering them!

Additional Resources:

Kingdom Parables by Christopher Lane (ages 4-8)
A First Look at God by Lois Rock (ages 4-8)

@ 8: Real Life Responsibility

Family Night
TOOL CHEST

Exploring responsibility in our families

Scripture:
• Matthew 25:14-30—The parable of the talents.

ACTIVITY OVERVIEW		
Activity	Summary	Pre-Session Prep
Activity 1: Carry On	Complete an obstacle course with a load of blocks.	You'll need building blocks, watch with second hand, paper, and pencil.
Activity 2: Growing Our Gifts	Explore ways to use gifts responsibly.	You'll need a Bible.

Main Points:

—We must learn how much responsibility we can handle.

—God wants us to act responsibly with whatever He gives us.

—We are only managers of what belongs to God.

LIFE SLOGAN: "Responsibility is learned and earned, one step at a time!"

69

Make it your own
In the space provided below, outline the flow and add any additional ideas to guide you through the process of conducting this family night.

Prayer & Praise Items
In the space provided below, list any items you wish to pray about or give praise for during this family night session.

Journal
In the space provided below, capture a record of any fun or meaningful things which happened during this family night session.

WARM-UP

Open with Prayer: Begin by having a family member pray, asking God to help everyone in the family understand more about Him through this time. After prayer, review your last lesson by asking these questions:

• **What do you remember from our last lesson?**
• **Do you remember the Life Slogan?**
• **Have your actions changed because of what we learned? If so, how?** Encourage family members to give specific examples of how they've applied past learning.

Share: Today we're going to learn about something that's important in life—being responsible.

ACTIVITY 1: Carry On

Point: We must learn how much responsibility we can handle.

Supplies: You'll need building blocks, a watch with second hand, paper, and pencil.

Activity: Have your family work together to create a obstacle course in your home. Your course might consist of crawling under a table, walking around a chair, and jumping over several toys. Let the children determine how simple or elaborate this will be.

When the course has been completed, have each family member make a "practice run" through the course. Time each person and record this time. Remember to go through the course yourself as well!

Share: In this game, we're all going to be racing against our own time. Don't worry if your time is slower than another family member. As we go through the course again, see if you can match or beat your own time. But this time let's make it a bit more challenging.

Activity continued: Give each person two of the building blocks. Explain that these must be carried while going through the course. Have everyone go through the

Age Adjustments

FOR OLDER CHILDREN, continue the discussion by having everyone list their regular responsibilities. Family members may be surprised as they realize what others actually accomplish each day. Take time to thank each other for the responsibilities carried each day that help others in the family. For example, children may thank Mom for all the driving she does for them, or a parent might thank a child for the regular dish-washing he does so everyone can eat on clean plates, and so on.

course again, making note of each person's time. Then add to the challenge by giving everyone two more blocks. Go through the course again and again, each time adding two more blocks to each person's load. Don't suggest this to children, but if they figure out creative ways to carry the blocks such as tucking them into belts or stowing them in pockets, that's okay.

Continue with this as long as family members are having fun, or until you run out of blocks! Then put the blocks away and gather together again for discussion. Look over your time record and see which runs through had the best times.

Question:
- **How did carrying the blocks affect your ability to go through the obstacle course?** *(Usually, the more blocks, the harder to handle the course.)*
- **What was the best way to get yourself and the blocks through the course?** *(Let all share.)*
- **When did you start to feel like you couldn't handle any more blocks?**

Share: Now let's discuss what this game has to do with our lives. Imagine your day as an obstacle course. Every time you add a responsibility to your day, it's like adding a block.

Discuss:
- **What responsibilities do you have each day?** *(Let family members list things like jobs, chores, studies, caring for pets, etc.)*
- **How are these like blocks as you go through the day?** *(They can become a lot to handle.)*
- **When do you feel like you're carrying too many blocks?**
- **Do you think you should be trying to carry more blocks of responsibility through each day, or less? Explain.**
- **How do we learn to be responsible?** *(We take on new responsibilities and explore how to handle them as we grow.)*
- **How do we get someone to trust enough to show we can be responsible?** *(We need to prove ourselves faithful in small tasks before we can take on larger ones.)*

ACTIVITY 2: Growing Our Gifts

Point: We need to act responsibly with whatever God gives us.

 Supplies: You'll need a Bible.

Read Matthew 25:14-30 together, then ask your children to summarize the story. If necessary, explain that a talent was a sum of money worth more than a thousand dollars.

Question:

- **Why did the one man hide what his master had given him?** *(He was afraid of losing it.)*
- **How could he have better used what his master had entrusted to him?** *(He could have used it to earn more.)*

Discuss: What if I were the master in this story, and I gave each of you two dollars to manage while I went away for a week. How could each of you act responsibly with that money and make it earn something for me?

Together think of how each person could make their two dollars grow. A child might use her two dollars to purchase yarn and make friendship bracelets to sell to her friends and thus make several more dollars. An older child might buy two dollars worth of gas for the lawn mower and cut grass for neighbors, charging enough to replace the gas and earn a profit. Help children think creatively.

If your budget permits, actually give each family member two dollars to make this discussion a reality. Be sure to include all adults (like yourself!) in this activity as well. Determine what you'll use the profits of this activity for ahead of time. Considering the topic of responsibility, you might like to give the money to a local charity, purchase items for a mission, or use it for another charitable activity.

After you've discussed how to act responsibly with money, **share: This story talks only of being responsible with money. Now we've already talked about all the responsibilities we each have, but let's focus more on what God has given us to be responsible with.**

Age Adjustments

FOR YOUNGER CHILDREN, read the story of the talents from a children's Bible story book. Even when children are young, they can learn the importance of acting responsibly with their toys and other belongings.

OLDER CHILDREN may enjoy learning about the stock market. Consider allowing them to make a small investment of money with the understanding that the profits will go to a chosen charity. Help them research their choices before making an investment. If you can't afford to actually invest at this time, let older kids choose a company to follow and see how much they could earn by their choice. Discuss what different people think are wise uses of money and what the pros and cons are of these uses.

• **What things has God given you to be responsible for?**

Answers to this question will vary depending on the age of your children. If kids need help on this one, suggest friends God has given, the money from their allowances, special abilities such as musical talent or a sharp mind, or even the responsibility to care for a pet. Be sure to mention *your* God-given responsibility as a parent to care for the gift of your children!

- **Just as we should be responsible with money, how can we be responsible with these things God's trusted us with?** (*We spend time and energy on them, perhaps giving up other activities.*)
- **Do you think you're being responsible with these things now?**
- **Have you proven through your actions that you're responsible with what others trust you with? Explain.**
- **How could you show more responsibility?** (*Be positive and encouraging here!*)

WRAP-UP

Gather everyone in a circle and have family members take turns answering this question: What's one thing you've learned today?

Next tell kids you've got a new "Life Slogan" you'd like to share with them.

Life Slogan: Today's Life Slogan is this, "Responsibility is learned and earned, one step at a time!" Have family members repeat the slogan two or three times to help them learn it. Then encourage them to practice saying it during the week so they can talk about it at your next family night session.

Close in Prayer: Allow time for each family member to share prayer concerns and answers to prayer. Then close your time together with prayer for each concern. Thank God for listening to and caring about us.

Remember to record your prayer requests so you can refer to them in the future as you see God answering them!

Additional Resources:

Money Matters (a board game by Rainfall Toys)
My Giving Bank (Rainfall Toys)
Short Cuts by Sigmund Brouwer (ages 8-12)

9: When Your Tongue Does the Talking

Exploring the power of our words

Scripture:
- James 3:3-12—The tongue is small but powerful.
- Proverbs 15:28—Evil hearts say evil words.
- Luke 6:45—Good comes from the heart of the good.
- Ephesians 4:29—Use words for building up others.

ACTIVITY OVERVIEW		
Activity	Summary	Pre-Session Prep
Activity 1: Strong Words	Compare the power of fire to the power of words.	You'll need a video or pictures of fire damage, a match, a candle and a Bible.
Activity 2: Take That Back!	Discover the permanence of spoken words.	You'll need tubes of toothpaste, paper plates, and a $10 bill.
Activity 3: Source of Speech	Look for the source of our words.	You'll need a Bible.

Main Points:

—The tongue is small but powerful.

—We can't take back the damage of our words.

—Our words reveal our heart.

LIFE SLOGAN: "Do it God's way—watch what you say!"

Make it your own
In the space provided below, outline the flow and add any additional ideas to guide you through the process of conducting this family night.

Prayer & Praise Items
In the space provided below, list any items you wish to pray about or give praise for during this family night session.

Journal
In the space provided below, capture a record of any fun or meaningful things which happened during this family night session.

WARM-UP

Open with Prayer: Begin by having a family member pray, asking God to help everyone in the family understand more about Him through this time. After prayer, review your last lesson by asking these questions:

- **What do you remember from our last lesson?**
- **Do you remember the Life Slogan?**
- **Have your actions changed because of what we learned? If so, how?** Encourage family members to give specific examples of how they've applied past learning.

Share: Today we'll be exploring what it means to control our tongues!

ACTIVITY 1: Strong Words

Point: The tongue is small but powerful.

Supplies: You'll need a video, news magazine or picture book showing the devastation of fire. Check your local library for video or pictures of a forest fire or a fire that destroyed many homes. You'll also need a match, a candle, and a Bible.

Activity: With your family, look at the video or pictures you've gathered. Then light the candle and discuss these questions by its light:

- **How did this huge fire we've learned about get started?**
- **How does one little flame like this one here cause so much damage?**
- **We've seen how much damage fire can cause. What good things can fire do?** (*Forest fires often clear out dead and diseased trees so that new ones have room to grow.*)
- **Can you think of any part of our bodies that can do a lot of good, or a lot of evil?**

Share: We can use many parts of our bodies for good or bad, but the Bible talks about one part specifically.

 Read James 3:3-12 aloud, then discuss:

- **What is the body part that can do so much good and so much bad?** (*The tongue.*)
- **Why do you think our tongues are so powerful?** (*The words they create can build up or tear down other people.*)
- **How are our tongues like a bit to an animal or a rudder to a ship?** (*A bit and a rudder are small things—like the tongue—but when handled properly, they have the power to change the course of a large animal or a ship.*)
- **What does it mean to tame your tongue, and why does the Bible say no one can do this?** (*We should learn to control our words, but our words spring from our hearts which should be under God's control.*)

Age Adjustments

FOR YOUNGER CHILDREN, say the rhyme, "Sticks and stones may break my bones but words can never hurt me."

Then ask: IS THIS TRUE? HOW DO YOU FEEL WHEN SOMEONE CALLS YOU A NAME OR TEASES YOU?

Explain that even though words are small, they still hurt!

CHILDREN OF ALL AGES may enjoy a trip to a local fire department on the day of this lesson. Call ahead to make appropriate arrangements with the staff. Many fire departments have everyday items such as toasters, telephones or toys which have been destroyed by fire. Examining these can further demonstrate the power of a tiny flame to grow and destroy. After you visit, discuss the same power our words have to grow and destroy.

Share: Just like fire can be used for good and for bad, our tongues can be used for good and for bad. Let's think of all the bad ways we use our tongues.

This list might include teasing, gossip, swearing, name-calling and telling lies.

Share: Now let's think of good ways we can use our tongues.

This list might include complimenting others, teaching, encouraging, comforting, and sharing about God.

 Question:
- **When was a time when someone's words made you feel bad?**
- **When was a time when someone's words made you feel good?**

Share: Our words can hurt or help.

ACTIVITY 2: Take That Back!

Point: We can't take back the damage of our words.

 Supplies: You'll need a tube of toothpaste for each child, paper plates and a $10 bill.

Activity: Give each child a tube of toothpaste and a paper plate. Instruct them to empty their tubes of toothpaste onto the plates.

Let kids have fun making swirls, towers, and other designs with the toothpaste. If you like, have a race to see who can empty their tube first.

Then place the $10 bill in the center of the table and explain: **You have three minutes. The first person to put all their toothpaste back into the tube wins the ten dollars. Go!**

(Parents, your money is safe. There's no way to get all the toothpaste back into the tube!)

After the three minutes put the money back in your pocket, throw away the tubes, toothpaste and paper plates and wash any hands that need it.

Discuss:
- **Which was harder, squeezing the toothpaste out, or putting it back in? Why?**
- **How is this like words coming out of our mouths?** (Once those words are spoken, we can't "unspeak" them; we can't take them back.)
- **When have you wished you could take back words you'd already said? What happened when you couldn't?**

Age Adjustments

FOR YOUNGER CHILDREN, go outside and blow soap bubbles for fun. Then ask the children to bring the popped bubbles back to you. Of course they can't, as the soap has evaporated into the air. Explain that our words are the same. Once we've said them they're gone. We can't collect them and put them back into our mouths.

Share: When we use our words to hurt others, we can apologize, but we can never take back what we said. It's hard to forget when someone has said a mean thing.

ACTIVITY 3: Source of Speech

Point: Our words reveal our heart.

Supplies: You'll need a Bible and a small mirror.

Activity: Take turns looking at each others' tongues and using the mirror so each person can look at his or her own tongue.

Question:

- **Can you see where the good or bad words come from when you look at your tongue or your throat?** *(No, we can't see the source of the words.)*
- **Where do words come from?** *(Our minds and hearts expressing our thoughts and feelings.)*

Share: Even though our throats and mouths form the words, the words really come from our minds. We say what we're thinking. The Bible explains this more.

 Read Proverbs 15:28 and Luke 6:45 aloud and discuss:

- **What do these verses mean?** *(Evil thoughts result in evil words, but good thoughts create good words.)*
- **What can you tell about a person by the way he or she talks?** *(You can learn about the heart from the words spoken.)*
- **Have you ever avoided becoming friends with a person because of the way that person talked? Explain.**
- **Imagine that a blind person came to have dinner with us. By only listening to our words, what would that person be able to tell about us? Are we a rude family? An encouraging family? A fighting family? A loving family?**

Share: Our words are a true reflection of what's in our hearts and minds. Since our minds control our tongues, we've got to learn to think before we speak! Another verse from the Bible tells us how God wants us to use our tongues.

 Read Ephesians 4:29 together and ask:

- **What kinds of words help others?** *(Words of praise and comfort, offers of help.)*
- **What kinds of words build up others?** *(Words like "thank you" and "you're special.")*
- **What kinds of words benefit those who hear them?** *(Words that instruct and guide.)*
- **How can we get more of these kinds of words into use**

here at our home? (*Let everyone share ideas and examine the ideas below.***)**

Activity continued: As a family, think of a way to be sure each person is encouraged with good words at least once a day for the next week. You might invent a game where each person gets a penny or nickel each time they encourage another family member. Or take time each evening at dinner to go around the table and build up family members. Or you might draw pictures of each other using words to describe how wonderful each family member is. Be creative and have fun finding a way to use your words for good!

WRAP-UP

Gather everyone in a circle and have family members take turns answering this question: What's one thing you've learned today?

Next tell kids you've got a new "Life Slogan" you'd like to share with them.

Life Slogan: Today's Life Slogan is this, "Do it God's way—watch what you say!" Have family members repeat the slogan two or three times to help them learn it. Then encourage them to practice saying it during the week so they can talk about it at your next family night session.

Close in Prayer: Allow time for each family member to share prayer concerns and answers to prayer. Then close your time together with prayer for each concern. Thank God for listening to and caring about us.

Remember to record your prayer requests so you can refer to them in the future as you see God answering them!

Additional Resources:

The Tattletale Tongue by Barbara Davoll (ages 4-8)
Night Light Tales by Andy Holmes (ages 4-8)

Age Adjustments

FOR YOUNGER CHILDREN, go into the kitchen or bathroom and turn on the faucet. See how clean the water is. Ask: DOES MUD EVER COME OUT INSTEAD OF WATER?

Explain that if dirty water ever came out of the faucet we'd know something was wrong in the well or water system. In the same way, if dirty or mean words come out of our mouths we know something is wrong in our hearts. Discuss how we can keep the words coming our of our mouths clean like the water coming from our pipes.

FOR OLDER CHILDREN, consider researching what it means to verbally abuse someone. See if you can find legal cases where people were punished for verbal abuse, or where it was a factor in a legal matter. You could also examine cases of libel and see what ramifications there are for lying about another person. Discuss how seriously people take the words others say about them. How does what we hear about ourselves change how we think about ourselves? Why don't we want others to hear bad things about us? What can we do to be sure we don't hurt others? How does having Jesus in our lives help us keep our hearts and minds clean?

@ 10: Just Say No!

Exploring how God helps us resist temptation

Scripture:
- Luke 4:1-13—Jesus is tempted.
- James 1:13-14—We're not tempted by our own evil desires, not by God.
- 1 John 2:15-17—Sources of temptation come from the world.
- 1 Corinthians 10:12-13—God provides a way our of temptation.
- James 4:7—Resist the devil.

ACTIVITY OVERVIEW		
Activity	**Summary**	**Pre-Session Prep**
Activity 1: Fishing for Trouble	Try to avoid temptation during a task.	You'll need a fishing pole, and items to use as bait as described in the lesson.
Activity 2: Just Like Jesus	Learn how Jesus dealt with temptation.	You'll need a Bible, paper, and crayons.
Activity 3: Scripture Stop Signs	Find verses to help resist temptation.	You'll need a Bible.

Main Points:

—Temptation takes our eyes off God.

—Even Jesus was tempted.

—We must resist temptation and focus on God

LIFE SLOGAN: "When tempted, say no and go—FLEE!"

Make it your own

In the space provided below, outline the flow and add any additional ideas to guide you through the process of conducting this family night.

Prayer & Praise Items

In the space provided below, list any items you wish to pray about or give praise for during this family night session.

Journal

In the space provided below, capture a record of any fun or meaningful things which happened during this family night session.

WARM-UP

Open with Prayer: Begin by having a family member pray, asking God to help everyone in the family understand more about Him through this time. After prayer, review your last lesson by asking these questions:

- **What do you remember from our last lesson?**
- **Do you remember the Life Slogan?**
- **Have your actions changed because of what we learned? If so, how?** Encourage family members to give specific examples of how they've applied past learning.

Share: Controlling our tongues takes a lot of effort. Today we'll be learning about something else that can take a lot of effort—resisting temptation!

ACTIVITY 1: Fishing for Trouble

Point: Temptation takes our eyes off God.

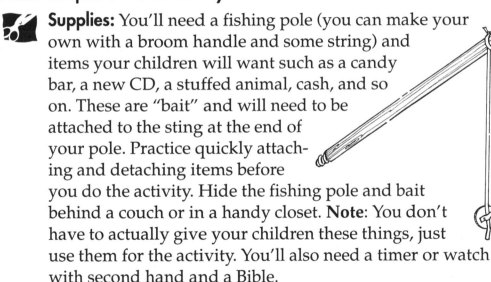

Supplies: You'll need a fishing pole (you can make your own with a broom handle and some string) and items your children will want such as a candy bar, a new CD, a stuffed animal, cash, and so on. These are "bait" and will need to be attached to the sting at the end of your pole. Practice quickly attaching and detaching items before you do the activity. Hide the fishing pole and bait behind a couch or in a handy closet. **Note**: You don't have to actually give your children these things, just use them for the activity. You'll also need a timer or watch with second hand and a Bible.

Activity: Choose a place in your home that has a large number of items that can be counted. For the ease of giving directions in this activity, we'll say this place is a brick fireplace, but in your home it might be a tile floor or counter, a long row of books on the bookshelf or a pile of toys. Have all family members except yourself sit with their backs to the fireplace.

Explain: **Everyone must keep looking away from the fireplace. I'll give each person a chance to turn around and count the bricks on the fireplace. You'll have two minutes to see how many you can actually count. You'll have to stay seated and count out loud.**

Set the timer, then ask one child to turn around and face the fireplace. (You may want to have the child move a foot or two further away from the fireplace so the other children won't have to turn their heads to see what's happening.)

Immediately pull out the fishing pole and drop one of the bait items in front of the face of the person counting. Swing the item around, tempting and teasing the child with it.

If the child stops counting or becomes distracted, allow the child to start counting again, but don't stop the time. When time's up, move on to another child. You may want to change the bait between kids, choosing what's most likely to distract that child.

If a child is not distracted, keep tempting until the two minutes are up, then move on to another family member.

When each child has had a turn at counting, put away the fishing pole and bait.

Age Adjustments

YOUNGER CHILDREN may not understand the four categories of temptation. Focus on the first part of the activity with them, discussing what things tempt them to do wrong. For example, when are you tempted to tell a lie? When are you tempted to hit your brother? When you know what is right to do, what tempts you to do wrong?

FOR OLDER CHILDREN further your discussion of this analogy for temptation by going over these "steps" of temptation:

1. The "bait" is dropped (such as the candy).

2. We take our eyes off God and place them on the bait (like when the focus turned from the counting to the candy).

3. We give in to temptation (try to take the candy).

4. We have a brief pleasure (eat the candy).

5. We feel guilty for failing or sinning when we realize what happened (the timer goes off, you're penalized for stopping counting, or realize you blew the assignment).

Discuss how temptations in our day to day lives follow these steps, and determine where temptation stops and sin starts.

Discuss:

• **Did anyone get the correct and final count?** (*It would be tough with all the distractions!*)

• **If you were distracted, what happened?**

• **If you weren't distracted, how did you keep your focus? What kind of bait might have caused you to look away?**

• **The bait was to tempt you from your task. What is temptation?** (*Something that pulls us off the right course or task.*)

• **What kinds of things tempt us in real life?** (*Let all share ideas.*)

Share: When you were counting, something was dropped before you to take your eyes off your job. Satan does the same thing by putting things before us that take our eyes off of following God. There are four categories of temptation—prestige, power, possessions and pleasure. These are the reasons we're tempted to do wrong things. Let's see how many temptations we can think of for each category.

Activity: If you like, make a list of the temptations your family thinks of. For example:

PRESTIGE

- Temptation to cheat on a test in order to have the best grade in class.
- Temptation to embarrass someone else so you look better to your friends.

POWER

- Temptation to lie about a co-worker so your boss gives you the promotion.
- Temptation to hit a younger brother or sister so you get your way.

POSSESSIONS

- Temptation to steal so we can have something we want.
- Temptation to be selfish with what we have instead of sharing.

PLEASURE

- Temptation to use alcohol or illegal drugs to make us feel better.
- Temptation to watch television instead of going to church.

ACTIVITY 2: Just Like Jesus

Point: Even Jesus was tempted.

 Supplies: You'll need a Bible, paper and crayons.

Share: Just like we're tempted each day, Jesus was tempted too.

 Read the account of Jesus being tempted in Luke 4:1-13.

Discuss:
- **How many times was Jesus tempted?** *(Three.)*
- **What were each of the temptations?** *(Food, earthly power, the chance to be like God.)*
- **Why was the devil trying to tempt Jesus?** *(To destroy His work.)*

• **How did Jesus respond in each situation?** *(He said no and answered out of God's Word.)*

Share: The devil tempted Jesus with food and power. Every time, Jesus quoted from the Bible to avoid the temptation. How would this work for us?

Activity: After discussion, give each family member a sheet of paper and place the crayons where all can share them.

Explain: **Draw a picture of you being tempted, or of something that is tempting to you. Whatever you draw, be sure it's something that really does tempt you.**

Be sure family members choose something that is an actual, realistic temptation for them. This might be food for a dieter, cheating for a student, or speeding for a driver.

When everyone (including yourself) is done drawing, take turns letting each person explain his or her drawing.

Discuss:
• **When are you most likely to be tempted?**
• **What ways do you try to avoid this temptation?**
• **How successful are you at avoiding this temptation?**
• **How do you think Jesus would avoid this temptation?**

ACTIVITY 3: Scripture Stop Signs

Point: We must resist temptation and focus on God.

 Supplies: You'll need a Bible.

 Read the following verses, discussing the questions after each verse.

James 1:13–14
• **What is tempting us?** *(Our evil desires; sin.)*
• **How does temptation drag us away?** *(We follow that which we desire; it looks too good to resist.)*
• **When do you feel like you're being dragged away from God or from what right?** *(Let all share.)*

1 John 2:15–17
• **How does loving the world lead us to temptation and sin?** *(We put the things of the world ahead of the things of God.)*

- Verse 16 give three broad categories of temptations from the world: cravings, lust of the eyes, and boasting. **What are specific temptations that fall into these categories?** *(Answers might include cravings for too much candy and junk food, desires for an expensive toy, the wish to appear better or smarter than others.)*

- **How do these temptations take us away from God?** *(They make us think things and achievements will bring more satisfaction than following God.)*

1 Corinthians 10:12–13

- **What does this passage mean to you?** *(God provides a way out of evil.)*

- **What ways does God provide for you to resist temptation?** *(It may be a person who helps, our own willpower, or reminders of His Word.)*

- **Do you honestly think you've ever been tempted more than you could handle?** *(Let all share.)*

- **How do you feel knowing God provides a way out of temptation?** *(It should give us strength.)*

- **Do you ever see the way out but choose to ignore it? If so, why?** *(Sometimes we selfishly want to go our own way; we think we won't get hurt.)*

James 4:7

- **How do we submit ourselves to God?** *(We ask Him to take charge of our lives and actions.)*

- **What happens when we resist the devil and his temptations?** *(The devil leaves us alone; he runs away.)*

- **Why do you think this happens?** *(God's power is greater than any power the devil may have.)*

Share: Now that we've looked at all these verses from the Bible, we know more about temptation and how to deal with it. Think about how these verses could help you deal with a temptation you face.

Age Adjustments

FOR YOUNGER CHILDREN, read this Bible account from a Bible storybook.

FOR OLDER CHILDREN, create a drama based on Luke 4:1-13. There are three parts: Jesus, the devil, and a narrator. If each member of your family has the same translation, you can use the Bible as your script, with each of the players reading the appropriate part.

If you like, dress the people playing Jesus and the devil in costumes. "Jesus" could wear a sheet as a robe, and "the devil" could wear all black, or you may think of other creative costumes.

After the performance from the Bible, act out ways we can resist the devil today. This role-playing can help children and adults practice realistic ways to resist things that tempt them in real life.

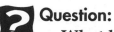
Question:
- **What kind of help does the Bible offer you on dealing with this temptation?** *(Try to think of specific passages to apply.)*
- **God said He won't tempt you more than you can handle, and will provide a way out. What's the way out of this temptation?** *(Let all try to offer ideas.)*
- **How can you resist this temptation?**
- **How does focusing on God help us resist temptation?** *(It gives us hope and strength.)*

Share: Jesus was able to resist the devil and temptation by quoting scripture. Scripture was sort of like a stop sign to temptation and sin. Jesus stayed focused on what God wanted, not what He wanted.

Activity: Have each person think of a verse they could use as a "stop sign" when they are tempted in order to bring their focus back to what God wants them to do.

Age Adjustments

FOR YOUNGER CHILDREN, the discussion in this section is too long. Focus on finding verses as stop signs to help younger children resist their specific temptations. This might be a verse such as Ephesians 4:29 for children who are tempted to say mean things, Ephesians 4:32 for those tempted to be selfish, and so on.

A concordance may help lead you to verses dealing with specific temptations. Proverbs is full of short passages offering good advice on right living; for example, if a family member is tempted by food, Proverbs 23:20-21 might be helpful. If lust is a problem, Proverbs 6:25-26 could be a good verse to remember. If you simply cannot find a Bible verse dealing with the temptation of a family member, use one of the verses from the previous discussion as an encouragement to turn away from the temptation.

If you did the previous activity, family members could draw stop signs on their pictures of things they are tempted by, with the verse they chose written in the sign.

Share: Jesus was able to use the Bible as his defense against temptation. Hopefully these verses will help us stop before we sin, and turn our focus back to what's right. Keep this picture for a week, putting it someplace where you can see it every day to help remind you of it's message.

WRAP-UP

Gather everyone in a circle and have family members take turns answering this question: **What's one thing you've learned about God today?**

Next tell kids you've got a new "Life Slogan" you'd like to share with them.

Life Slogan: Today's Life Slogan is this, "When tempted, say no and go—FLEE!" Have family members repeat the slogan two or three times to help them learn it. Then encourage them to practice saying it during the week so they can talk about it at your next family night session.

Close in Prayer: Allow time for each family member to share prayer concerns and answers to prayer. Then close your time together with prayer for each concern. Thank God for listening to and caring about us.

Remember to record your prayer requests so you can refer to them in the future as you see God answering them!

Additional Resources:

The White Trail by Barbara Davoll (ages 4-8)
Kids Choices (Rainfall Toys, ages 6-12)
How to Be Your Own Selfish Pig by Susan Macauly (ages 8 and up)

@ 11: The Friendship Factor

Exploring the importance of choosing good friends

Scripture:
- John 15:1-8—Parable of the vine and the branches.
- Matthew 7:15-20—Wolves in sheep's clothing.

ACTIVITY OVERVIEW		
Activity	Summary	Pre-Session Prep
Activity 1: Branch Out!	Compare a branch to a Christian.	You'll need a tree branch, pencils, paper, and a Bible.
Activity 2: Friend in a Bag	Learn that outside looks don't tell us what's on the inside.	You'll need ten paper sacks, ten small items, a marker, and a Bible.
Activity 3: Encouraging Friends	Thank good friends for their friendship.	You'll need art supplies.

Main Points:

—The friends we choose can tear us away from God, or help us stay close to God.

—We can't choose friends by their looks. Instead, we must know what's inside.

—Be thankful for the good friends you have.

LIFE SLOGAN: "Choose a friend by his fruit, not by his suit!"

Personal
NOTES

Make it your own
In the space provided below, outline the flow and add any additional ideas to guide you through the process of conducting this family night.

Prayer & Praise Items
In the space provided below, list any items you wish to pray about or give praise for during this family night session.

Journal
In the space provided below, capture a record of any fun or meaningful things which happened during this family night session.

 WARM-UP

   Open with Prayer: Begin by having a family member pray, asking God to help everyone in the family understand more about Him through this time. After prayer, review your last lesson by asking these questions:

- **What do you remember from our last lesson?**
- **Do you remember the Life Slogan?**
- **Have your actions changed because of what we learned? If so, how?** Encourage family members to give specific examples of how they've applied past learning.

Share: Sometimes the people who tempt us are our own friends! That's why we're going to explore how important it is to choose our friends carefully.

ACTIVITY 1: Branch Out!

Point: The friends we choose can tear us away from God, or help us stay close to God.

 Supplies: You'll need a tree branch, paper and pencils, and a Bible.

Activity: Give each person a paper and pencil. Explain: **Write down the qualities you look for in a friend.**

   Have older family members help those who can't yet write. Then have family members set these papers aside for a few minutes.

   Hold out the tree branch and ask:

- **From this branch, what can you tell me about the tree it came from?** (*Most will observe the branch looks like the tree from which it came.*)
- **Will this branch grow anymore? Why not?** (*The branch will not grow because it is cut off from its food source.*)

Share: The branch can't grow because it's broken away from the tree. Jesus once talked about branches when he was talking with his followers.

   Read John 15:1-8 aloud, then ask:

- **What are the four key parts or people in this story?** (*Vine, branch, fruit, gardener*)
- **What does each of these represent?**

(In your discussion, be sure the following points are made:)

Vine: This is the trunk that gives life to the branch. It represents Jesus Christ, who give us eternal life.

Branch: The branch produces fruit, but can't produce fruit if it's apart from the vine. It represents us and other Christians who have a relationship with God. Like the branch is attached to the vine, we are attached to God.

Fruit: Any fruit growing on a tree grows from the branch. The fruit represents qualities of Christlikeness such as the fruit of the Spirit (Galatians 5:22-23), or obedience, justice, and righteousness as referred to in another similar parable in Isaiah 5:1-7.

Gardener: A gardener cares for the trees. He trims away dead branches and throws them into the fire, and prunes the growing branches so more life will go toward growing new fruit.

In the same way God "prunes" or disciplines Christians so we can become more Christlike and grow more "fruit."

Age Adjustments

YOUNGER CHILDREN may not understand the whole branch analogy. Explain it to them as simply as possible. They will, however, be able to tell if certain friends are more likely to help them get into trouble or stay out of trouble. Discuss which friends are better to have, and what can be done to help those who lead your child into trouble. Is it worth having this friendship if it leads your child astray?

Discuss:

- **What does this story say we should be doing if we, like the branch, are attached to the vine, meaning God?** *(We should show the "fruit" in our lives—Christlike qualities.)*

- **What are some of the characteristics you think other people see in you that shows you're like Christ?** *(We try to be loving and obey God's commandments.)*

- **Now look at your paper where you listed what you look for in a friend. How many of these qualities are ones that reflect being like Christ?**

- **Do you think it's important to have strong Christians as friends? Why or why not?** *(Strong Christian friends help us stay strong.)*

- **How can a friend pull us away from God, and keep us from growing "good fruit" ? Would a person like this be a true friend?** *(We might end up trying to act like our friend, instead of following Jesus' example.)*

- **What kind of friend helps us get closer to God? How does a friend do this?** *(A true friend helps us grow "good fruit" by setting a good example in thoughts, words, and deeds.)*

- **Which kind of friend do you want to have—one that helps**

you grow, or one that tears you away from God? Explain.
- Do you think the friends you have now are "attached to the vine"? How can you tell?

ACTIVITY 2: Friend in a Bag

Point: We can't choose friends by their looks. Instead we must know what's inside.

 Supplies: You'll need ten paper sacks, a marker, ten small items, and a Bible. Before your time together, place the small items in different paper sacks, and number each bag from one to ten. Set these aside until you're ready to use them.

Activity: Bring out the sacks you've prepared ahead of time. Explain: **Reach into each sack and feel what's inside. Don't peek! Just feel the item, then use the blank side of your qualities of friendship paper to write down what you think is in the bag.**

For children who can't yet write, have an adult help, or pair older children and younger children into teams with the older child doing the writing.

When everyone's had a chance to feel inside all ten bags, have family members read off their first entry, then empty the first bag to see who was correct. Continue down the list until everyone's shared their findings and the true contents of each sack has been revealed.

Discuss:
- **By looking at the outside of each sack, was there any way to tell what was inside?**
- **Did you have any trouble figuring out what was inside each bag when you could put your hand inside? Explain.**

 Read Matthew 7:15-20, then discuss:

- **Can you choose a friend by how he or she looks? Explain.** *(People are not always the same inside as they appear outside.)*
- **What kind of person dresses like a sheep but inside is a ferocious wolf?** *(Some people are fake—pretending to be what they aren't.)*

- **This verse talks about good fruit coming from good people. What does this mean?** (*Good actions and deeds come from those who truly love God.*)
- **Have you ever had a friend, or known someone, that looked good on the outside, but turned out to be bad inside? Explain.**
- **How is this like guessing what's on the inside of these bags?** (*We can't know someone based only on outward appearance.*)
- **What's the best way to choose a friend?** (*We need to spend time with them and see how they act during different situations, to understand how they really are.*)

Share: We couldn't tell what was inside the bags without reaching in and touching what was there. In the same way, we can't tell what's on the inside of people until we feel or see their actions. You may meet someone who's handsome and dresses nicely, but turns out to be a liar. On the other hand, you might meet someone who is unattractive, or looks rough, but find out through their actions they love Jesus just like you do!

We've got to listen to what people say and see what they do. Then we can know whether they're true friends who will help us stay close to God, or if they're really wolves in disguise who are leading us away from God and into trouble.

Age Adjustments

FOR YOUNGER CHILDREN, help them think of friends who help them do good and make them feel loved. Let children make cards for these friends, thanking them and encouraging them for their gift of friendship.

FOR OLDER CHILDREN, read *The Giving Tree* by Shel Silverstien (check your local library) and discuss what kind of friendship this is. Are they more like the boy or the tree? Is this true friendship or a one-sided friendship? Does this story remind them of any of their friends? Is that good or bad?

ACTIVITY 3: Encouraging Friends

Point: Be thankful for the good friends you have.

Supplies: You'll need a Bible and art supplies such as construction paper, scissors, glue, and markers.

This activity is a supplement to Activities One and Two in this section.

Activity: Tell your family to look back at the qualities they wrote down earlier. They should cross out any that they don't think are as important anymore, and add any that they now think of as important. When everyone has done this, explain: **Now go through this list of quali-**

ties and think of one of your friends who demonstrates this quality in your friendship. For example, if honesty is on your list, you might think of a friend who has always told you the truth. If faithfulness is on your list, you might think of a friend who has never gossiped about you or who stood beside you and believed in you when others didn't. If you've named a quality that fits none or your friends, leave it blank.

When everyone has completed their lists, take time for each person to share about his or her friends.

Share: A true friend wants us to grow closer to God, helps us, loves us, and encourages us. We should let our true friends know how much we appreciate them, and encourage them back!

Activity: Use the construction paper, glue, scissors, and other craft supplies to create cards of encouragement to one or more friends. Have family members be sure to tell their friends, through the cards, what qualities they especially appreciate about them. Mail or deliver the cards right away!

WRAP-UP

Gather everyone in a circle and have family members take turns answering this question: **What's one thing you've learned about God today?**

Next tell kids you've got a new "Life Slogan" you'd like to share with them.

Life Slogan: Today's Life Slogan is this, "Choose a friend by his fruit, not by his suit!" Have family members repeat the slogan two or three times to help them learn it. Then encourage them to practice saying it during the week so they can talk about it at your next family night session.

Close in Prayer: Allow time for each family member to share prayer concerns and answers to prayer. Then close your time together with prayer for each concern. Thank God for listening to and caring about us.

Remember to record your prayer requests so you can refer to them in the future as you see God answering them!

Additional Resources:

Daisy Doddlepaws and the Windy Woods Treasure by Michael Waite (ages 4-8)
Hot Chocolate Friendship by Nancy Simpson Levene (ages 8-12)
In Grandma's Attic by Arleta Richardson (ages 8-12)

☺ 12: One Bad Apple?

Exploring how non-Christians can lead us away from God

Scripture:
- 1 Corinthians 15:33—Bad company corrupts good character.
- 2 Corinthians 6:14–7:1—Don't be yoked with unbelievers.

ACTIVITY OVERVIEW		
Activity	Summary	Pre-Session Prep
Activity 1: Unequally yoked	Unmatched pairs move toward different goals.	You'll need a small ball, paper, pencil, yarn or tape, and a Bible.
Activity 2: Just a Drop	Discover the effect of a small amount of sin.	You'll need a Bible, milk, and food coloring.
Activity 3: Cut it Out!	Examine current friendships for strengths and weaknesses.	You'll need paper, scissors, pencils, and a Bible.

Main Points:

—Christians and non-Christians have different goals and purposes in life.

—Evil is contagious.

—We may need to end relationships that are leading us away from God.

LIFE SLOGAN: "Don't be a loser, be a Good Friend Chooser!"

Make it your own
In the space provided below, outline the flow and add any additional ideas to guide you through the process of conducting this family night.

Prayer & Praise Items
In the space provided below, list any items you wish to pray about or give praise for during this family night session.

Journal
In the space provided below, capture a record of any fun or meaningful things which happened during this family night session.

 WARM-UP

Open with Prayer: Begin by having a family member pray, asking God to help everyone in the family understand more about Him through this time. After prayer, review your last lesson by asking these questions:

- **What do you remember from our last lesson?**
- **Do you remember the Life Slogan?**
- **Have your actions changed because of what we learned? If so, how?** Encourage family members to give specific examples of how they've applied past learning.

Share: Having good friends is such an important topic that we're going to continue learning about it now!

ACTIVITY 1: Unequally Yoked

Point: Christians and non-Christians have different goals and purposes in life.

Supplies: You'll need a ping pong ball or other small ball, slips of paper, pencil and yarn or masking tape. Before your time together write "A" or "B" on all the slips of paper. You should have about four or five of each letter. Fold the slips and place them in a cup or other container. Use the yarn or masking tape to create two equally sized circles on the floor. Circles should be about as big as a dinner plate. Place a small paper beside one circle designating it as Circle A, and another paper labeling the other Circle B.

Activity: Have family members form pairs (or trios, depending on the number of people in your family). Have each person draw a slip of paper from the cup and look at it *without letting the partner know what is on the slip.*

Explain: **The goal in this game is to blow this ball into the circle matching the letter you just drew. You've got to work with your partner to blow the ball into your circle, but don't tell your partner which circle you're working toward.**

Let the first pair try the activity. Obviously, if they both drew the same letter, they'll quickly blow the ball into the appropriate circle.

Otherwise, they'll be working against each other. Don't comment on this, just let family members have fun trying to get the ball into their circles. Then let another pair or trio have their turn. Be sure to join in the fun yourself! After everyone has had a turn, form new pairs or trios, draw new slips of paper, and play again as often as family members want.

Discuss:
- **When was it easy for you to get the ball into your goal?**
- **What made it difficult?**

Share: When we drew different letters, we weren't working with each other, we were working against each other. Let me read a passage in the Bible that talks about this.

 Read 2 Corinthians 6:14-16 and question:

- **What does it mean to be yoked with someone?** *(Attached to them in a strong relationship—such as marriage.)*
- **What would it mean to be equally yoked or unequally yoked?** *(If they are equally yoked, the people are pulling in the same direction; if not they would move in opposite directions.)*
- **How can you answer some of the questions in this passage?** *(The things being compared are opposites.)*

Share: Our game demonstrates what this means. When you were with a partner that had the same goal in mind, you were equally yoked. Because you were working together toward the same goal, it made the job easier. But when you and your partner had different goals, you were unequally yoked. Instead of working together, you were fighting your partner, and only one of you could win.

Discuss:
- **How is our game like friendships?** *(We should all strive for friendships where the people involved share the same goal.)*
- **How do our friends help us toward our goal of being like God, or lead us away from that goal?** *(They can influence us by their actions and examples.)*
- **This verse talks about not being yoked with people who aren't Christians. What does that mean?** *(While we can be friends with non-Christians, we need to be careful about those relationships and the activities we do with those friends.)*

- **Why do you think it's important to God that we don't be yoked, or in relationships, with people who aren't Christians?** *(We don't want to be in a position where non-Christian friends have a strong influence on our choices and behavior.)*

Share: We usually like to have friends that have something in common with us. Think about the friends you have now. What things do you have in common? Often friendships form and last because we have something in common with others. Why is it important the our friends have the common goal of loving God?

Share: We've seen from our game that being unequally yoked can lead us in the wrong direction.

ACTIVITY 2: Just a Drop

Point: Evil in contagious.

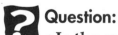 **Supplies:** You'll need a small glass of milk and a dark color of food coloring such as green or red.

Activity: Place the glass of milk where everyone can see it. Let one drop of food coloring drop into the water, gently stir and watch what happens.

Question:
- **Is the milk still white? What happened?**
- **Can we make the milk white again?**
  If you like, add a few more drops and stir, watching as the milk gets darker and darker.

Share: This is a very simple way to show us that even one drop of sin can change us.

Discuss:
- **How does sin change us?** *(Sin changes our hearts so that our thoughts and actions tend to not honor God.)*

Age Adjustments

OLDER CHILDREN may enjoy a variation on this game. Instead of blowing balls, form pairs for a three-legged race. Again, draw letters indicating which finish line you're running toward, and see if pairs go toward the same goal or fight to go toward different goals. Use the same line of questioning, making the point that only one person can win when there are different goals, and it's not so fun fighting with your partner instead of being helped by your partner.

- **If we keep sinning, how is that like adding more drops of coloring into the milk?** *(The more sin, the more it shows in out choices and actions.)*
- **How can having non-Christian friends add sin to our lives?** *(If we choose to follow their leading instead of God's, it can result in sinful choices.)*

 Read 2 Corinthians 6:17-7:1 and discuss:

- **This is the rest of the passage about being unequally yoked with unbelievers. How do these verses relate to our experiment?** *(Like the food coloring changes the milk, our relationships change our hearts.)*
- **What kind of friends does God want us to choose and why?** *(Friends who make right choices can help us make right choices too.)*
- **What kind of people does He want us to avoid and why?** *(People who choose to sin can lead us into sin. We might see them do something wrong and want to do the same.)*
- **What kinds of bad influences do you think a person your age could tempt you with?** *(Let everyone share.)*
- **Why would you want to have a friend who was leading you toward the wrong goal?**

Age Adjustments

FOR OLDER CHILDREN, discuss how, even though we Jesus forgives our sins, it's hard to forget them. For example, if we hear a bad word from friends, we don't have to say it ourselves, but we'll still remember that word in our minds. It's a way sin contaminates us. Or if we watch an inappropriate movie, we can be forgiven, but the images we watched will stay in our minds. See if your children can think of other ways sin sticks with us.

Share: Jesus can forgive us for sinning. If we use our milk as an example, Jesus could make the milk white again. But it's better if we don't sin in the first place! Just as the color spread through the milk, sin spreads. We want to avoid sin and need to be careful in our friendships with people who aren't Christians. We don't want to be influenced by their wrong ideas or choices. Instead, we want to be a positive influence on others!

ACTIVITY 3: Cut it Out!

Point: We may need to end relationships that are leading us away from God.

 Supplies: You'll need paper, pencils, tape, and scissors.

Activity: Give each family member paper, a pencil and scissors. Using the guide on page 108, cut out a row of paper people.

Have family members write their own names on the center person.

Explain: **Think of your two closest friends, and write their names on the other two people "attached" to you. Then write ways this person leads you on their figure. For example, if a friend tries to get you to smoke cigarettes, skip classes, or tell a lie, write that on their figure. If a friend enjoys going to church with you, or demonstrates qualities of a Christian as we've discussed in the past, write those things on that figure. You may even have a mixture of good and bad things on the same person.**

Younger children may need an older family member to help think of and write the appropriate comments on their figures.

 Read 1 Corinthians 15:33, and discuss.

Share: Now look at yourself and the two people to whom you're attached. In reality, you are attached to others by your friendship or relationship with them.

 Question:
- **How could you be misled?** *(The wrong friend could lead you into sin.)*
- **How do you think bad company can corrupt good character?** *(Getting you involved in wrong activities.)*
- **Considering what you've written on their figures, do you think either or both of these people are leading you toward or away from God? Explain.** *(Encourage all to share.)*
- **Does it seem that either of these people might try to change you in a way you believe is wrong? If so, how?**
- **Are you in bad company that is corrupting you?**

Age Adjustments

FOR YOUNGER CHILDREN, discuss when it's best to not play with another child who influences your child toward wrong-doing. This might be a child who is rude or disrespectful to adults, or who cheats when playing games with your child. Help your child understand that it's okay to not play with this child, and sometimes it's better to play alone than have to deal with this kind of "friendship."

FOR OLDER CHILDREN, further your discussion of how to end a relationship that's leading in the wrong direction. When is it better to stop trying to change someone and just admit they're changing you more than you're helping them? How can using wisdom in choosing friends help you to avoid having to end bad relationships? If you're "stuck" in a relationship (a teacher pairs you in seating or a project, the person is a fellow employee you must work with, and so on), how can you best avoid being "contaminated" by the other person? How can you "contaminate" them with God's love instead? How does this topic of friend and sin relate to Mark 9:42-49? How do we distance ourselves from those who cause us to sin or encourage us to sin?

Piece of paper for dolls.

Fold paper in an accordion fold.

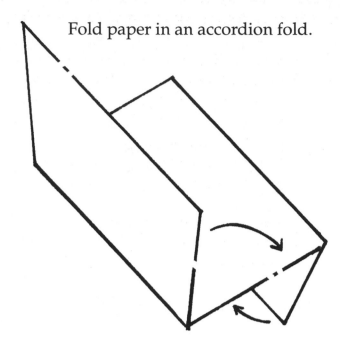

Lightly draw the shape of your doll on the front panel. Make sure hands touch both edges of panel.

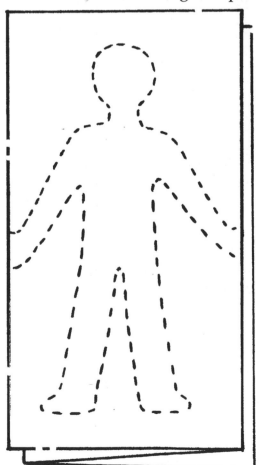

After cutting along your lines, you should be able to open folded dolls and get three dolls holding hands.

Share and question: If you see that a friendship is misleading you, tear that paper person off to show an ending of that relationship.

- If you do this, how will you better be able to follow God.
- Ending a friendship isn't as easy as just tearing a piece of paper. How can we end friendships in a kind way?
- If you tore a friend off, how will you seek to end that relationship in real life?
- What person could you seek as a friend that will help you on your goal of being like Jesus?

Share: We don't have to turn our backs on these people. We can still pray for them and try to be examples of God's love. But we don't have to let them influence what we do by spending a lot of time with them.

Take a minute now to pray for people who seem to be bad influences on members of your family. Pray that God would change their hearts and bring them to Him, and that they would no longer try to lead others toward wrong.

WRAP-UP

Gather everyone in a circle and have family members take turns answering this question: **What's one thing you've learned about God today?**

Next tell kids you've got a new "Life Slogan" you'd like to share with them.

Life Slogan: Today's Life Slogan is this, "Don't be a loser, be a Good Friend Chooser!" Have family members repeat the slogan two or three times to help them learn it. Then encourage them to practice saying it during the week so they can talk about it at your next family night session.

Close in Prayer: Allow time for each family member to share prayer concerns and answers to prayer. Then close your time together with prayer for each concern. Thank God for listening to and caring about us.

Remember to record your prayer requests so you can refer to them in the future as you see God answering them!

Additional Resources:

Bibleland Game (Rainfall Toys, ages 4-8)
You Too Can Know Jesus (Chariot Books, ages 4-8)

ⓔ How to Lead Your Child to Christ

SOME THINGS TO CONSIDER AHEAD OF TIME:

1. Realize that God is more concerned about your child's eternal destiny and happiness than you are. "The Lord is not slow in keeping his promise.... He is patient with you, not wanting anyone to perish, but everyone to come to repentance" (2 Peter 3:9).

2. Pray specifically beforehand that God will give you insights and wisdom in dealing with each child on his or her maturity level.

3. Don't use terms like "take Jesus into your heart," "dying and going to hell," and "accepting Christ as your personal Savior." Children are either too literal ("How does Jesus breathe in my heart?") or the words are too clichéd and trite for their understanding.

4. Deal with each child alone and don't be in a hurry. Make sure he or she understands. Discuss. Take your time.

A FEW CAUTIONS:

1. When drawing children to Himself, Jesus said for others to "allow" them to come to Him (see Mark 10:14). Only with adults did He use the term "compel" (see Luke 14:23). Do not compel children.

2. Remember that unless the Holy Spirit is speaking to the child, there will be no genuine heart experience of regeneration. Parents, don't get caught up in the idea that Jesus will return the day before you were going to speak to your child about salvation and that it will be too late. Look at God's character—He *is* love! He is not dangling your child's soul over hell. Wait on God's timing.

    Pray with faith, believing. Be concerned, but don't push.

THE PLAN:

1. **God loves you.** Recite John 3:16 with your child's name in place of "the world."

2. **Show the child his or her need of a Savior.**

   a. Deal with sin carefully. There is one thing that cannot enter heaven—sin.

   b. Be sure your child knows what sin is. Ask him to name some (things common to children—lying, sassing, disobeying, etc.). Sin is doing or thinking anything wrong according to God's Word. It is breaking God's Law.

   c. Ask the question "Have you sinned?" If the answer is no, do not continue. Urge him to come and talk to you again when he does feel that he has sinned. Dismiss him. You may want to have prayer first, however, thanking God "for this young child who is willing to do what is right." Make it easy for him to talk to you again, but do not continue. Do not say, "Oh, yes, you have too sinned!" and then name some. With children, wait for God's conviction.

   d. If the answer is yes, continue. He may even give a personal illustration of some sin he has done recently or one that has bothered him.

   e. Tell him what God says about sin: We've all sinned ("There is no one righteous, not even one," Rom. 3:10). And because of that sin, we can't get to God ("For the wages of sin is death . . . " Rom. 6:23). So He had to come to us (". . . but the gift of God is eternal life in Christ Jesus our Lord," Rom. 6:23).

   f. Relate God's gift of salvation to Christmas gifts—we don't earn them or pay for them; we just accept them and are thankful for them.

3. **Bring the child to a definite decision.**

   a. Christ must be received if salvation is to be possessed.

   b. Remember, do not force a decision.

   c. Ask the child to pray out loud in her own words. Give her some things she could say if she seems unsure. Now be prepared for a blessing! (It is best to avoid having the child repeat a memorized prayer after you. Let her think, and make it personal.)*

d. After salvation has occurred, pray for her out loud. This is a good way to pronounce a blessing on her.

4. **Lead your child into assurance.**

Show him that he will have to keep his relationship open with God through repentance and forgiveness (just like with his family or friends), but that God will always love him ("Never will I leave you; never will I forsake you," Heb. 13:5).

* If you wish to guide your child through the prayer, here is some suggested language.

"Dear God, I know that I am a sinner [have child name specific sins he or she acknowledged earlier, such as lying, stealing, disobeying, etc.]. I know that Jesus died on the cross to pay for all my sins. I ask you to forgive me of my sins. I believe that Jesus died for me and rose from the dead, and I accept Him as my Savior. Thank You for loving me. In Jesus' name. Amen."

Cumulative Topical Index

TOPIC	SCRIPTURE	WHAT YOU'LL NEED	WHERE TO FIND IT
The Acts of the Sinful Nature and the Fruit of the Spirit	Gal. 5:19-26	3x5 cards or paper, markers and tape	Book 1, p. 43
All Have Sinned	Rom. 3:23	Raw eggs, bucket of water	Book 2, p. 89
Bad Company Corrupts Good Character	1 Cor. 15:33	Small ball, string, slips of paper, pencil, yarn or masking tape, Bible	Book 1, p. 103
Be Thankful for Good Friends		Bible, art supplies, markers	Book 1, p. 98
Christ Is Who We Serve	Col. 3:23-24	Paper, scissors, pens	Book 1, p. 50
The Consequence of Sin Is Death	Ps. 19:1-6	Dominoes	Book 2, p. 57
Creation	Gen. 1:1; Ps. 19:1-6; Rom. 1:20	Nature book or video, Bible	Book 1, p. 17
David and Bathsheba	2 Sam. 11:1–12:14	Bible	Book 2, p. 90
Description of Heaven	Rev. 21:3-4, 10-27	Bible, drawing supplies	Book 2, p. 76
Don't Be Yoked with Unbelievers	2 Cor. 16:17–17:1	Milk, food coloring	Book 1, p. 105
Don't Give Respect Based on Material Wealth	Eph. 6:1-8; 1 Peter 2:13-17; Ps. 119:17; James 2:1-2; 1 Tim. 4:12	Large sheet of paper, tape, a pen, Bible	Book 1, p. 64
Evil Hearts Say Evil Words	Prov. 15:2-8; Luke 6:45; Eph. 4:29	Bible, small mirror	Book 1, p. 79
The Fruit of the Spirit	Gal. 5:22-23; Luke 3:8; Acts 26:20	Blindfold and Bible	Book 2, p. 92
God Allows Testing to Help Us Mature	James 1:2-4	Bible	Book 2, p. 44
God Created Us	Isa. 45:9; 64:8; Ps. 139:13	Bible and video of potter with clay	Book 2, p. 43
God Forgives Those Who Confess Their Sins	1 John 1:9	Sheets of paper, tape, Bible	Book 2, p. 58
God Gave Jesus a Message for Us	John 1:14, 18; 8:19; 12:49-50	Goldfish in water or bug in jar, water	Book 2, p. 66

TOPIC	SCRIPTURE	WHAT YOU'LL NEED	WHERE TO FIND IT
God Is Holy	Ex. 3:1-6	Masking tape, baby powder or corn starch, broom, Bible	Book 1, p. 31
God Is Invisible, Powerful and Real	John 1:18; 4:24; Luke 24:36-39	Balloons, balls, refrigerator magnets, Bible	Book 1, p. 15
God Knew His Plans for Us	Jer. 29:11	Two puzzles and a Bible	Book 2, p. 19
God Knows All About Us	Ps. 139:2-4; Matt. 10:30	3x5 cards, a pen	Book 2, p. 17
God Knows Everything	Isa. 40:13-14; Eph. 4:1-6	Bible	Book 1, p. 15
God Loves Us So Much, He Sent Jesus	John 3:16; Eph. 2:8-9	I.O.U. for each family member	Book 1, p. 34
God Made Our Family Unique by Placing Each of Us in It		Different color paint for each family member, toothpicks or paintbrushes to dip into paint, white paper, Bible	Book 2, p. 110
God Made Us in His Image	Gen. 1:24-27	Play dough or clay and Bible	Book 2, p. 24
God Provides a Way Out of Temptation	1 Cor. 10:12-13; James 1:13-14; 4:7; 1 John 2:15-17	Bible	Book 1, p. 88
God Wants Us to Get Closer to Him	James 4:8; 1 John 4:7-12	Hidden Bibles, clues to find them	Book 2, p. 33
God Will Send the Holy Spirit	John 14:23-26; 1 Cor. 2:12	Flashlights, small treats, Bible	Book 1, p. 39
God's Covenant with Noah	Gen. 8:13-21; 9:8-17	Bible, paper, crayons or markers	Book 2, p. 52
The Holy Spirit Helps Us	Eph. 1:17; John 14:15-17; Acts 1:1-11; 1:8; Eph. 3:16-17; Rom. 8:26-27; 1 Cor. 2:11-16; Eph. 1:17	Bible	Book 2, p. 99
Honor Your Parents	Ex. 20:12	Paper, pencil, treats, umbrella, soft objects, masking tape, pen, Bible	Book 1, p. 55
The Importance of Your Name Being Written in the Book of Life	Rev. 20:11-15; 21:27	Bible, phone book, access to other books with family name	Book 2, p. 74
It's Important to Listen to Jesus' Message		Bible	Book 2, p. 68

TOPIC	SCRIPTURE	WHAT YOU'LL NEED	WHERE TO FIND IT
Jesus Dies on the Cross	John 14:6	6-foot 2x4, 3-foot 2x4, hammers, nails, Bible	Book 1, p. 33
Jesus Took the Punishment We Deserve	Rom. 6:23; John 3:16; Rom. 5:8-9	Bathrobe, list of bad deeds	Book 1, p. 26
Jesus Washes His Followers' Feet	John 13:1-17	Bucket of warm, soapy water, towels, Bible	Book 1, p. 63
Joshua and the Battle of Jericho	Josh. 1:16-18; 6:1-21	Paper, pencil, dots on paper that when connected form a star	Book 1, p. 57
The More We Know God, the More We Know His Voice	John 10:1-6	Bible	Book 2, p. 35
Nicodemus Asks Jesus about Being Born Again	John 3:7, 50-51; 19:39-40	Bible, paper, pencil, costume	Book 2, p. 81
Obedience Has Good Rewards		Planned outing everyone will enjoy, directions on 3x5 cards, number cards	Book 1, p. 59
Parable of the Talents	Matt. 25:14-30	Bible	Book 1, p. 73
Parable of the Vine and Branches	John 15:1-8	Tree branch, paper, pencils, Bible	Book 1, p. 95
The Responsibilities of Families	Eph. 5:22-33; 6:1-4	Photo albums, Bible	Book 2, p. 101
Serve One Another in Love	Gal. 5:13	Bag of small candies, at least three per child	Book 1, p. 47
Sin Separates Humanity	Gen. 3:1-24	Bible, clay creations, piece of hardened clay or play dough	Book 2, p. 25
Some Places Aren't Open to Everyone		Book or magazine with "knock-knock" jokes	Book 2, p. 73
Some Things in Life Are Out of Our Control		Blindfolds	Book 2, p. 41
Temptation Takes Our Eyes Off God		Fishing pole, items to catch, timer, Bible	Book 1, p. 85
Those Who Don't Believe Are Foolish	Ps. 44:1	Ten small pieces of paper, pencil, Bible	Book 1, p. 19
The Tongue Is Small but Powerful	James 3:3-12	Video, news magazine or picture book showing devastation of fire, match, candle, Bible	Book 1, p. 77

TOPIC	SCRIPTURE	WHAT YOU'LL NEED	WHERE TO FIND IT
We All Sin	Rom. 3:23	Target and items to throw	Book 1, p. 23
We Can Communicate with Each Other			Book 2, p. 65
We Can Help Each Other	Prov. 27:17	Masking tape, bowl of unwrapped candies, rulers, yardsticks, or towel rods	Book 2, p. 110
We Can Love by Helping Those in Need	Heb. 13:1-3		Book 1, p. 48
We Can Show Love through Respecting Family Members		Paper and pen	Book 1, p. 66
We Can't Take Back the Damage of Our Words		Tube of toothpaste for each child, $10 bill	Book 1, p. 78
We Deserve Punishment for Our Sins	Rom. 6:23	Dessert, other materials as decided	Book 1, p. 24
We Have a New Life in Christ	John 3:3; 2 Cor. 5:17	Video or picture book of caterpillar forming a cocoon then a butterfly or a tadpole becoming a frog or a seed becoming a plant	Book 2, p. 93
We Know Others by Our Relationships with Them		Copies of questionnaire, pencils, Bible	Book 2, p. 31
We Must Choose to Obey		3x5 cards or slips of paper, markers and tape	Book 1, p. 43
We Must Learn How Much Responsibility We Can Handle		Building blocks, watch with second hand, paper, pencil	Book 1, p. 71
We Reap What We Sow	Gal. 6:7	Candy bar, Bible	Book 1, p. 55
With Help, Life Is a Lot Easier		Supplies to do the chore you choose	Book 2, p. 101
Wolves in Sheeps' Clothing	Matt. 7:15-20	Ten paper sacks, a marker, ten small items, Bible	Book 1, p. 97
You Look Like the Person in Whose Image You Are Created		Paper roll, crayons, markers, pictures of your kids and of yourself as a child	Book 2, p. 23

About
Heritage Builders

OUR VISION

To build a network of families, churches, and individuals committed to passing a strong family heritage to the next generation and to supporting one another in that effort.

OUR VALUES

Family—We believe that the traditional, intact family provides the most stable and healthy environment for passing a strong heritage to the next generation, but that non-intact homes can also successfully pass a solid heritage.

Faith—We believe that many of the principles for passing a solid heritage are effective regardless of one's religious tradition, but that the Christian faith provides the only lasting foundation upon which to build a strong family heritage.

Values—We believe that there are certain moral absolutes which govern our world and serve as the foundation upon which a strong heritage should be built, and that the current trend toward value neutrality is unraveling the heritage fabric of future generations.

Church—We believe that all families need a support network, and that the local church is the institution of choice for helping families successfully pass a strong heritage to the next generation.

OUR BELIEFS

We embrace the essential tenets of orthodox Christianity as summarized by the National Association of Evangelicals:

1. *We believe the Bible to be the inspired, the only infallible, authoritative Word of God.*

2. *We believe that there is one God, eternally existent in three persons: Father, Son, and Holy Ghost.*

3. We believe in the deity of our Lord Jesus Christ, in His virgin birth, in His sinless life, in His miracles, in His vicarious and atoning death through His shed blood, in His bodily resurrection, in His ascension to the right hand of the Father, and in His personal return in power and glory.

4. We believe that for the salvation of lost and sinful people regeneration by the Holy Spirit is absolutely essential.

5. We believe in the present ministry of the Holy Spirit by whose indwelling the Christian is enabled to live a godly life.

6. We believe in the resurrection of both the saved and the lost; they that are saved unto the resurrection of life and they that are lost unot the resurrection of damnation.

7. We believe in the spiritual unity of believers in our Lord Jesus Christ.

OUR PEOPLE

Heritage Builders is lead by a team of family life experts.

Cofounder - J. Otis Ledbetter, Ph.D.
 Married over 25 years to Gail, two grown children, one teenager
 Pastor, Chestnut Baptist Church in Clovis, California
 Author - *The Heritage, Family Fragrance*

Cofounder - Kurt Bruner, M.A.
 Married over 12 years to Olivia, two young sons
 Vice President, Focus on the Family Resource Group
 Author - *The Heritage, Family Night Tool Chest* Series

Cofounder - Jim Weidmann
 Married over 15 years to Janet, two sons, two daughters
 Family Night Training Consultant
 Author - *Family Night Tool Chest* Series

Senior Associates - Heritage Builder draws upon the collective wisdom of various authors, teachers, and parents who provide resources, motivation, and advice for the heritage passing process.

BECOME A HERITAGE BUILDER IN YOUR COMMUNITY!

We seek to fulfill our mission by sponsoring the following.

HERITAGE BUILDERS RESOURCES - Products specifically designed to motivate and assist parents in the heritage passing process.

HERITAGE WORKSHOP - Using various formats, this seminar teaches attendees the principles and tools for passing a solid heritage, and helps them create a highly practical action plan for doing so.

HERITAGE BUILDERS NETWORK - A network of churches which have established an ongoing heritage builder support ministry where families can help families through mutual encouragement and creativity.

HERITAGE BUILDERS NEWSLETTER - We provide a forum through which families can share heritage building success stories and tips in our periodic newsletter.

If you are interested in hosting a Heritage Workshop, launching a Heritage Builders ministry in your local church, learning about new Heritage Building resources, receiving our newsletter, or becoming a Heritage Builder Associate, contact us by writing, phoning, or visiting our web site.

Heritage Builders Association
c/o ChariotVictor Publishing
4050 Lee Vance View
Colorado Springs, CO 80918
or call: 1-800-528-9489 (7 A.M.– 4:30 P.M. MST)
www.chariotvictor.com
or
www.heritagebuilders.com

HERITAGE BUILDERS

☐ Please send me a FREE One-Year Subscription to Heritage Builders Newsletter.

Name _____

Address _____

City _____ State _____ Zip _____ Phone _____

Church Affiliation _____

E-mail Address _____

Signature _____